THE DULAS VALLEY VICTORY

The Dulas Valley Victory

and the Tryweryn factor

Marian Harris

First publication: 2019

Published with the financial support
of the Welsh Book Council

ISBN: 978–1-84524-292-3

Cover design: Eleri Owen

Published by Gwasg Carreg Gwalch,
12 Iard yr Orsaf, Llanrwst, Wales LL26 0EH
tel: 01492 642031
email: books@carreg-gwalch.cymru
website: www.carreg-gwalch.cymru

Printed and published in Wales

*To my father Iorwerth Evans
and all those involved in this epic battle
to save our valley.*

Marian Harris was born and raised on a small farm in the Dulas Valley in Radnorshire, where in the late 1960's her family home, along with many others, came under threat from a proposed reservoir to provide for increasing water demands in England.

A few years previously, the residents of Capel Celyn in Merionethshire had been cruelly ejected from their homes when the Tryweryn valley was flooded.

Never has a single emotive word aroused as much passion throughout the Welsh nation as that of Tryweryn. Memories of that travesty still linger. For the people of the Dulas Valley, such memories were all too raw. They were determined to avoid the same fate, so irrepressibly took on the Severn River Authority as it then was. It was a gargantuan challenge, but they simply had no choice other than to fight to save their homes and community.

Marian is well placed to document both the events leading up to and the progress of the Public Inquiry, as at the time she was secretary to the solicitor acting in the case, whilst her father was Chair of the Defence Committee.

The narrative comes straight from the heart of someone totally immersed in her subject, with a determination that the facts should be recorded for posterity so that lessons may be learnt. It will appeal to anyone having the belief that 'people power' is paramount when faced with seemingly insurmountable odds - in this instance the threat of having their entire community annihilated.

Hopefully, the book will be appreciated by all who love this beautiful part of Wales and who nurture a belief that things like justice and fairness are well worth fighting for, if only to secure the legacy of a living and vibrant community for future generations.

Contents

The beauty of the Mid Wales landscape is legendary and should not be subjected to the whims of ill thought out, unfettered colonialism. It was not before time that the region should no longer suffer such wanton destruction. Someone had to make a stand.

Introduction

Throughout Wales there are innumerable streams and rivers carrying the name 'Dulas'. Why the name is so common I am not sure, but for me personally, it has great significance. *My* Dulas – and that of my brothers and sisters – was the river flowing through the Valley bordering our home farm. Each day we crossed the bridge to get to school. I can remember as a young girl always rushing across it, slightly doubtful of its safety. It was of course perfectly sturdy and secure, but I was blissfully unaware of the threat that lay ahead for its very existence, had a certain River Authority had its way.

The Dulas Valley where I was privileged to be born and raised bordered the old Counties of Montgomeryshire and Radnorshire. It is an area steeped in tradition and culture, with significant connections to Wales' rich historical past. Owain Glyndŵr, undoubtedly Wales' most iconic leader, was a frequent visitor to an old hall house at 'Cenarth', the home of his daughter Gwenllian and her husband, Philip ap Rhys. The house was at or near Bryncenarth, where my maternal grandparents lived and where I spent many happy hours as a child. There is no record of Owain's death and historians can only speculate in what plot of earth he was buried, but I am sure he would have been distraught at the prospect that his daughter's fertile lands should, centuries later, be drowned under fathoms of water. The very name *Glyndŵr* means 'the valley of water', and I like to think that Owain's spirit came back to haunt the promoters of this ill-conceived flooding scheme and, in the end, influenced the outcome. There is much we don't know, even if we think we do. Clearly *my* Cwm Dulas was not meant to be 'the valley of water' nor was it, like the enigmatic Glyndŵr, to disappear for ever from the face of the earth.

In December 1282, Llewelyn ap Gruffudd, the last legitimate native Prince of Wales, was fatally ambushed near the River Irfon outside Builth by English invaders. The natural spring of Prysg Duon rises near the Dulas Valley where Llewelyn's slayer washed his bloody hands. The prince's headless body was buried in the Abbey of Cwmhir to the east. As youngsters we were told that the English king, Edward I, ordered his men to convey Llewelyn's head to his castle at Rhuddlan and thence on to London. There it was paraded through the streets as a warning to all before being impaled at the Tower of London, mockingly decked with a crown of ivy. It was a symbol of Edward's power over 'the troublesome Welsh', a power which he sought to strengthen by crowning his new born son at Caernarfon under the usurped title of Prince of Wales.

We may not have been brought up with our mother tongue, but we were nevertheless very familiar with our history and our Welsh heritage. It meant a great deal to us, strengthening our feeling of *cynefin* – that most emotive of Welsh nouns meaning 'a sense of belonging'.

The Dulas Valley was very much ours. As with us all,

my life some forty years ago was turned upside down when we first heard about the proposals to drown our farms and our homes. None of us could possibly have imagined such a threat. The land, the buildings, the chapel, the graveyard, the river itself and the bridge we used to cross as children were to disappear under a huge reservoir to supply the industrial conurbations of the Midlands. Welsh valley communities had been lost before. Water was a highly sensitive issue throughout Wales.

Fortunately for us, the Severn River Authority's plans were defeated.

For many years I have wanted to catalogue the events leading up to these proposals and the battle that ensued. Other things got in the way. I was too involved with being a housewife and a mother, helping with the rebuilding of our house whilst holding down a part-time job, tending to our large garden and all the other commitments of the way of life in which I had been nurtured. I was involved in local politics and the activities of the schools my son attended. I was often either preparing for or going out to evening meetings.

Now that my life has become arguably less hectic in retirement, I decided that it was important to put pen to paper so that future generations would know what might have been lost. We had lived in our close-knit community all our lives and the last thing on our minds was the thought of anything happening to it. We led a sheltered life by the standards of today, but that in itself had its compensations. It is so important that these events are recorded for posterity.

The threat of losing our revered way of life was of even greater significance to me because my father became Chairman of the local Defence Committee, formed to defend the Valley. As I lived with my parents at the time, I witnessed the stress and responsibility he felt upon finding himself in that position. However, he took it all in his stride. He was soon comfortable in speaking to the many reporters who turned up at our home. When Gareth Morgan, a partner in Milwyn Jenkins and Jenkins, a local firm of solicitors, was instructed to act in the case, I became even more deeply involved as I was his secretary at the time. Inevitably, I was involved in the increasing amount of correspondence being generated.

Sometimes I became a target for complaints. I can clearly recall one instance when I received a telephone call from the Llanidloes Town Clerk on the first morning of the Public Inquiry. He told me that we had broken the fire regulations at our fund-raising concert the night before by overfilling the Community Hall! I avoided any great conversation on such a petty matter – I was just setting out to the Inquiry and that was uppermost in my mind. But on the whole, people were encouraging and helpful and their empathy boosted our efforts.

This factual account is, I hope, a reflection of the integrity, resilience and determination of a rural community whose very existence was under threat. A community, ostensibly disparaged by the Establishment, but by no means fearful of it, came together as one to fight its corner – and we were vindicated. David *did* defeat Goliath! It was the first time that a community had defeated a water authority's bid to flood a Welsh valley and it felt good. In a valley with such a strong musical tradition, the Inspector's ultimate decision was indeed music to our ears.

I have related a combination of what I recorded and what I can remember from my first-hand involvement, along with facts gleaned from various newspaper cuttings in my possession. I can only hope that the collating of all the information and events leading up to the Public Inquiry will illustrate how insecure our way of life might be. We all take our homes and our daily joys and chores for granted. My hope is that anyone taking the trouble to read this compilation will have a greater understanding of human nature in the face of mounting odds and seemingly unjust adversity.

Communities are made up of people. We should never forget that, when we take on vested interests and big business, People Power is paramount. It is to be hoped that my readers will bear that in mind and take it forward. We can all achieve wonders if we stick together, whatever odds we face. As that old saying declares 'There is strength in numbers.'

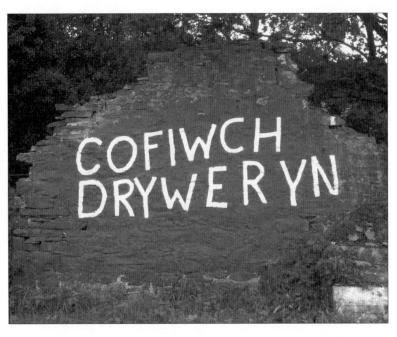

*One of the most memorable and recognizable images of Welsh
patriotism is the dramatic piece of graffiti initiated by Meic
Stephens, one of the significant literary giants of modern times,
commemorating the travesty of Tryweryn. Situated on the gable
end of a derelict cottage near Llanrhystud, Ceredigion and
dating from about the time of the Dulas Inquiry, it has since
become an icon of Welsh nationhood. The fact that this
monument is from time to time repainted ensures that Tryweryn
will never be forgotten. Memories linger in a small and closely
knit nation such as ours.*

Chapter One

The Threat

It was in 1966 that the Severn River Authority announced that they were proposing to investigate twenty-nine valleys in Montgomeryshire to ascertain their suitability for the building of a reservoir. The Dulas Valley was one of those named. We were not hugely concerned at that stage because we thought that the likelihood of us being chosen out of twenty-nine valleys seemed remote.

The Water Resources Act, 1963 provided for the establishment, in England and Wales, of twenty-nine river authorities charged with the duty of taking '. . . all such action as they may from time to time consider necessary and expedient, or as they may be directed to take by virtue of this Act, for the purpose of conserving, redistributing or otherwise augmenting water resources in their area, or of transferring any such resources to the area of another authority'. The Act set up a Water Resources Board '. . . charged with the duty of advising river authorities with respect to the performance of their new functions, and of advising the Minister with respect to the performance of his functions under Section 1 of the Water Act 1945'. In 1965, the then Secretary of State for Wales, James Griffiths, additionally set up a Welsh Water Committee to advise him on water matters in Wales.

In June 1965 Mr Griffiths instructed the Welsh Water Committee and the Severn River Authority to report on the future lines of development of the water resources of the Welsh part of the Upper Severn basin. Early the following year, the River Authority sought permission to survey twenty-nine valleys and in a letter to those affected, the Severn River Authority informed us that Messrs Binnie and Partners, Consulting Engineers, were carrying out investigations of possible reservoir sites on their behalf. Initially the investigations would consist of visual surveys of the land. They wrote:

'It may be necessary for representatives of the firm to enter on your land for this purpose within the next few weeks. If it is subsequently found necessary to carry out borings or trial pits a further letter will be sent to you. Some thirty different sites are being surveyed and it should be possible once the survey has been completed and the Consultants' report considered, to eliminate a number of the sites for some considerable period from any further investigation or consideration. I would emphasise that, unless I write to you again, entry on your land, if at all, will only be for the purpose of examining the general nature of the ground and should be possible without any damage or disturbance. Your co-operation will be greatly appreciated.'

The Severn River Authority claimed that the water would be needed by 1978 and that it had a statutory duty to provide for future water needs under the 1963 Water Resources Act. They were obviously looking for the cheapest option.

Of the twenty-nine sites, most of the land was in Montgomeryshire. There was a small amount in Denbighshire, but what affected *us* was land bordering Montgomeryshire and Radnorshire. This caused considerable disquiet amongst all who lived their lives at any of these sites. We knew we had to stick together and work out what we were to do. It seemed extremely unfair and illogical that homes and livelihoods in Mid Wales could be ruined, just so that the standard of living of another community could be improved.

Very soon the decision was reached that all the areas affected should meet.

On Friday 20 May 1966 at 7.30 pm, a meeting was convened at Llanfair Caereinon High School for all interested parties who had concerns about the issue of reservoir construction throughout the principality. A Mr E. F. Evans was nominated Chairman for that meeting. He welcomed everyone to the meeting and reminded them of what he called 'the serious tasks ahead'. The intention was that we would form a properly run committee which meant business. Those present immediately set about forming a constitution. An agenda was agreed and draft rules drawn up. The name of the committee was to be The Mid Wales (Reservoirs) Defence Committee and it was decided that the office and place of meeting would be 22 High Street, Newtown, or at any other place approved by the Committee.

The primary objectives were (a) to oppose in the first instance the construction of dams and reservoirs within Mid Wales which would be detrimental to the area and (b) to negotiate and secure adequate and fair compensation for displaced persons in the event of the scheme gaining approval and going ahead.

The membership of the Committee would consist of two representatives from each of the proposed dam and reservoir areas. Our Dulas Valley representatives were Gordon Pugh and my father, Iorwerth Evans. Officers appointed were Chairman: Mr Leslie Morgan (of the then

Development Board for Rural Wales); Secretary: Mr R. P. Davies (County Secretary of the Farmers Union of Wales) and Treasurer: a bank official working within the affected area.

The voting system and finance were discussed. The resolution stated that 'The Committee shall be dissolved

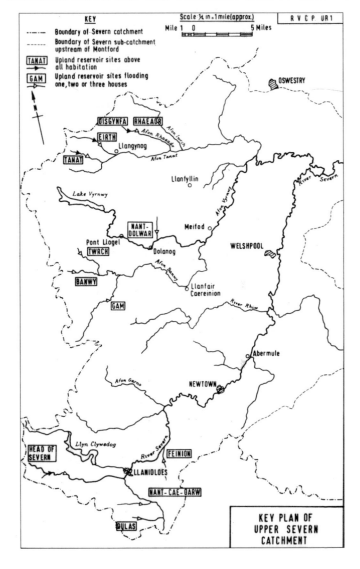

KEY PLAN OF
UPPER SEVERN
CATCHMENT

when all threats of building reservoirs have been removed from Mid Wales or at any time that the Committee may decide by special resolution.'

The affected sites were:

Ogau, Iwrch, Rhaeadr, Dulas, Banwy 1, Banwy 2, Banwy 3, Banwy 4, Banwy 6, Twrch, Lower Gam, Upper Gam, Wytham, Lower Fyrnwy, Upper Fyrnwy, Bechan, Mule, Rhiw 54/11, Rhiw, Severn 54/1, Upper Severn, Feinion, Trannon, Cerist, Alan, Cain, Nant Ffyllon, Tanat and Eirth.

Leslie Morgan, who took over the Chair, asked members of the Press who were in attendance to leave until the Committee had decided whether or not they should remain. It was proposed that they should be admitted but when put to the vote, the proposal was heavily lost and the Press were informed that a statement would be made later by the Chairman.

A Mr C. L. J. Humphreys of the Country Landowners Association, who was in attendance, was asked for his view of the situation. He said that the CLA wished to help the Committee, consistent with its policy applicable to other parts of the country. The CLA had advocated barrages lower down the rivers but believed that the demands for water in England and Wales must be satisfied. Also flood prevention must be considered: the establishment of three or four reservoirs might assist members down river. The CLA could not oppose outright the construction of dams, but they would press for the fullest compensation for those dispossessed. He said that the CLA felt that it was inadvisable at that moment to oppose the survey and considered it should go ahead. But they reserved the right to say which valleys should be drowned, based on factors which included the number of people affected.

It was decided that the Committee should elicit the support of the three Members of Parliament involved, namely Emlyn Hooson (Montgomeryshire) Tudor Watkins (Radnorshire) and W. Geraint Morgan (Denbighshire).

The Chairman, Leslie Morgan, closed the meeting by reminding its members that this was likely to be a long, hard fight against ludicrous and grotesque proposals made out of all reason. He said, 'We are not unreasonable people and the magnitude of the plan and its possibilities are the basic cause for alarm and concern.'

Emlyn Hooson raised the matter in an adjournment debate in the House of Commons on 27 May 1966. He said that he was grateful for the opportunity of raising the matter of the Severn River Authority's plans to survey twenty-nine valleys for their possible use as reservoirs, a matter of supreme importance to many of his constituents and to Wales generally. He said that he was sure that by now there was no need for him to try to persuade the House that Wales is devoted to its rural valleys and small communities; that there was little need to convince the Secretary of State of the fierce emotions which the threat of flooding a valley produces in the Principality.

'Why is it not possible for the Secretary of State to eliminate from the survey certain areas immediately on social, cultural and economic grounds? Some of the areas on the survey include whole communities threatened with flooding. It is time that the Secretary of State put his foot down. His appointment was welcomed by many of us who do not share his political views because we believe that he is devoted to the cause of Wales. It would be a salutary matter and a great benefit to Wales, to the River Authority and all concerned if he would make an authoritative statement today, setting out exactly what his views are and what is the official approach to this problem which I think will increase in size in the next few years in Wales. What consideration is the survey expected to give to Welsh cultural and social life? One of the fears of the people of Montgomeryshire has been the apparently clandestine nature of the negotiations leading up to the publication of the fact that the survey was being made.'

Mr W. G. Morgan (MP for Denbigh) followed in the debate and added that he would like an assurance from the Secretary of State, if it were possible for him to give it, that if it were to be found necessary to take another Welsh site at all, there would be the least possible disturbance to existing inhabitants.

In his reply, Mr Cledwyn Hughes said that he was concerned, as was his predecessor, that there should never be a repetition of controversy such as arose over Tryweryn. He continued:

'Let me say now, so that there may be no more misunderstanding or further misconception, that as Secretary of State for Wales I do not propose to consent to the drowning of any villages in Mid Wales. I am satisfied that if regulating reservoirs are required, then the two or three which I mentioned can be built without disrupting whole communities. I can assure the Honourable and Learned Gentleman Mr Hooson and the Honourable Gentleman the Member for Denbigh Mr W. Morgan that communities count as far as I am concerned.'

This sentiment was later confirmed by his successor, Mr George Thomas. It was to be the lynchpin of our case at the Inquiry.

The three MPs were invited to the next meeting of the Mid Wales Defence Committee on 3 June 1966. However, only Emlyn Hooson was able to attend and was invited to address the meeting. He immediately expressed his grave concern at the proposal. He dwelt on the history of events leading to the publication of the map which had been produced: '. . . an horrific document in itself because it purports to show by way of illustration, about one third of the land surface of Montgomeryshire under water.' He referred to the Secretary of State's remark in the Commons when he claimed 'I do not propose to consent to the drowning of any village in Mid Wales.' Emlyn Hooson did not regard the word *village* as requiring definition. 'Village is any community or cluster of houses, not necessarily having a church or chapel there' he said. The Secretary of State had also said in the House that '. . . the need for preserving first class agricultural land will also be very much in my mind' but Mr Hooson felt that in Wales there was a close link between good agricultural land and uplands. He said that he also felt that further research into the use of guttered land in the higher forestry areas should be undertaken, together with questions such as barrages at the mouths of rivers, coastal desalination plants etc. whilst remembering that there was no easy solution and that the cost of piping would always be high.

After much debate with Mr Hooson, the Chairman emphasised that the important factor was the wholehearted and unanimous support of the Committee in its endeavours.

On 13 June 1966, the Committee met representatives from the Severn River Authority and Binnie and Partners Consulting Engineers to discuss the *'elimination of valleys'* and for a question and answer session. Speaking for the Severn River Authority, a Colonel Goodman stated that the history of all this went back eight or nine years to the Central Advisory Water Committee which had been set up to estimate requirements over thirty to forty years and to quantify available water resources. Sub-committees had been formed to discuss these issues. After two years' work, the CAWC concluded that plenty of water was available, if it was properly conserved and not allowed to run into the sea. It reported to the Government which passed the Water Resources Act 1963 and had charged River Authorities to survey all resources of the area for which they were responsible. The Severn River Authority had been invited to make this survey because the Act demanded it. He said that the Severn River Authority was not committed to any particular sites. Any survey which involved the flooding of centres of population would be ruled out. The survey would help to decide which sites were suitable and which were not. He said there were four considerations in selecting sites:

(1)   geological suitability of the ground;
(2)   the least possible damage to human habitation;
(3)   the least possible damage to agricultural land;
(4)   the possibility that a site could be utilised for both water storage and flood alleviation.

Members of the Committee then put forward their questions, and discussions followed.

Meanwhile, in the Dulas Valley, a local defence committee was In the process of being set up. Gordon Pugh (then aged 41) had been appointed as Secretary and my sixty-year-old father, Iorwerth Evans, as Chairman. My father was very apprehensive about taking on this role as he felt ill equipped for the task and often, before a meeting, he was given a 'pep' talk by my mother because she knew he could undertake the job. He was an intelligent and level headed man and he and Gordon Pugh, a dependable character, would work together well.

On 8 July 1966 the Committee wrote to the Secretary of

State for Wales, Cledwyn Hughes:

'As representatives of the Dulas Valley Defence Committee we have been instructed to write to you protesting against the proposed water resources survey by the Severn River Authority in the Upper Dulas Valley and also throughout twenty-eight other sites in Mid Wales.

'This committee states that whilst realising the need for conservation of water, it nevertheless takes exception to the way the Severn River Authority has undertaken to make this survey with no prior notice or consultation other than direct notice to the people concerned.

'We understand that the River Board intends to build two or three dams within a specified period of time and as this particular area was classified "A" in the previous survey, there is considerable disquiet and alarm prevailing in this district.

'The whole life of our district will be affected from a religious, cultural and social aspect and in consequence we feel obliged to pursue a course of total opposition to the proposals as they now stand.

'This committee considers that the compensation terms payable under the Water Resources Act appear to be so inadequate to the individuals losing their homes or means of livelihood. Therefore we ask you to use your good offices to bring pressure to bear in government circles for a greater degree of compensation:

'We feel impelled to ask you:

Why Wales is again asked to stand another round of desecration?

Are other River Boards carrying out surveys of their water resources, as we cannot recollect ever seeing these facts reported in the national press?

'We trust you will favour us with an early reply.'

The Secretary of State announced in the House of Commons on 3 August 1966 that he had agreed to a survey of ten of the original twenty-nine sites put forward. The Water Resources Committee considered that any regulating reservoir to be constructed should provide sufficient water to meet foreseeable future demands and that the capacity of the reservoir should therefore be capable of yielding, at the very least, 100 million gallons per day. If the new reservoir was to be in operation by 1975, he said that it would be necessary to start work on its construction by 1970 and for its location to be chosen 'without further delay'.

When, in the House of Commons, Mr Gwynfor Evans MP questioned the Prime Minister Harold Wilson about the threat to Welsh water resources and supplies, the reply he received was

'There are always problems when natural water boundaries do not coincide with political and administrative boundaries. However, the biggest threat I can see to Welsh water resources is those who are always blowing them up!'

Such a crass and insensitive remark was, to say the least, totally inappropriate coming from a Prime Minister and had the effect of making us even more determined to fight our corner, using every ploy at our disposal.

The Mid Wales (Reservoirs) Defence Committee then met on 2 September 1966 to discuss this new development. The ten sites named were as follows:

Dulas (Upper) – upstream of Tylwch Halt; Dulas (Lower) – downstream of Tylwch Halt; Twrch – half a mile upstream of Foel village; Upper Vyrnwy – one mile upstream of Dolanog village; Upper Gam – four miles

upstream of Llanerfyl village; Eirth – one mile upstream
of Llangynog village; Tanat – half a mile upstream of
Llangynog village; Head of Severn (Upper) – within
area of Hafren Forest; Head of Severn (Lower) – half a
mile downstream of Glynhafren; Mule – one mile
upstream of Abermule.

The Committee decided that even though there were only
ten sites now affected, the whole committee should remain
intact and support the people who lived at those sites.

As far as opinions within the Dulas Committee were
concerned, Gordon Pugh stated that they were prepared to
co-operate with the survey rather than take any violent
unconstitutional or illegal action – but if the survey could
be avoided they would be so much the happier. Iorwerth
Evans added that they were not totally committed to co-
operate, but rather that if the worst came to the worst they
would do so. They felt that perhaps the site in the upper
reaches of the Valley was feasible.

The Severn River Authority's Consultants however,
were denied access to these sites. They would have to
report on the results of assessments made from public
rights of way and from desk studies and calculations.

The next move was that the Mid Wales (Reservoirs)
Defence Committee set up a sub-committee. Iorwerth
Evans was chosen to serve on it. When asked for
comments from the Dulas Committee, he stated that it
would not be too bad if the Authority concentrated on the
deep gullies up to the 900-feet mark because there was no
good land there but rather rocks and deep ravines. Higher
up however, the land flattened out into a productive
plateau, a good stock rearing area. He also felt that regard
should be paid to the culture of the area. Although the
community was not a Welsh speaking one, he maintained

that Welsh culture was deeply ingrained throughout. It was actively fostered and supported; the spirit of that Welsh culture and associations was very much alive and would be threatened if a reservoir project came about. There was also the religious and educational aspect. The proposal would affect two chapels with a membership of about a hundred and a local school.

In the meantime The Mid Wales Sub-committee received a letter from Gwynfor Evans, Plaid Cymru MP for Carmarthen, offering assistance to carry out a petition among electors in the county against the Reservoirs Survey Plan. A discussion followed. The Chairman thought that the Committee would obviously be grateful for the offer of any assistance, but wondered whether enlisting the support of one party alone would show political bias. Iorwerth Evans was against the incursion of politics into the issue. The Chairman felt that if a petition was necessary, then the Defence Committee itself should organise it. However, he felt that the time was not yet ripe for such a move and it was resolved to recommend to the main Mid Wales Defence Committee to delay it.

On 14 January 1967 the Mid Wales Defence Committee met the Secretary of State for Wales, Cledwyn Hughes. Alderman Tudor Watkins and Emlyn Hooson were present. Mr Hooson was in the Chair and after he had introduced the Secretary of State, Mr Hughes confirmed that he had reduced the number of sites from twenty-nine to ten. He hoped to satisfy the Committee of the need to co-operate on the stages up to the 'reservoir' stage, namely visual inspection, investigative boring, the holding of a Public Inquiry and then his decision. He stated that having ten sites did not mean that there would be ten reservoirs; the aim was for one reservoir followed by another two or three in the next twenty years. He believed that goodwill on all sides would enable the plans to go ahead. He asked the Committee to co-operate with the authorities and promised to look after the interests of Wales and individuals. Mr Leslie Morgan asked, in relation to the two or three additional reservoirs in twenty years, where in fact was it likely to end? His concern was that as demand for water increased, so would the need for further reservoirs and that the threat would remain or even increase. He pressed for other forms of water conservation.

After this meeting the Secretary of State held a press conference where he said he would be pressing the Minister of Agriculture and his colleagues in the Government for action to improve the rate of compensation for tenant farmers. The position then current was that a tenant farmer might be compensated with a sum equivalent to five years' rent. No allowance would be made for the very low rent payable where a family had farmed the land for many years. For such tenants to set up farming somewhere else would be virtually impossible.

The main Mid Wales Defence Committee met again on 25 January 1967 to discuss their reaction to the request by the Secretary of State for Wales that visual inspection of the sites named in the list of ten should proceed. Some members favoured permission to allow the surveys to go ahead, whilst others were totally against it. Gordon Pugh said that the Dulas Committee was prepared to co-operate with the visual survey. He said that they favoured co-operation because if the Severn River Authority made a substantial bid for land and property, older people might wish to sell out and settle elsewhere. He further made it clear that both he and Iorwerth Evans would be personally affected. Other members of the Defence Committee however, whilst respecting the views of the Dulas

Committee, still felt that they should not co-operate. Iorwerth Evans explained that the Montgomeryshire Local Authority had not supported the Committee.

The Chairman concluded that with a few exceptions, the feeling of the Committee was to decline to co-operate. However, in summing up, the onus was put on local committees to devise their best methods of opposition. If guidance was needed, the advice of the Mid Wales Defence Committee could be sought. He suggested that each site nominate one person on the telephone who would act as liaison between his Committee and the Secretary of the local committee. Following this meeting, a letter was written to the Secretary of State informing him of the Committee's decision not to co-operate with the visual inspection of sites. This letter stated:

'You will, we are aware, be disappointed that we have come to this conclusion, but we are anxious that you should believe that it has not been reached lightly, nor without the most careful consideration of the possible advantages that might flow from co-operation. The Committee was particularly aware that an early inspection should perhaps remove the cloud of uncertainty from a number of valleys and that a full survey of the remaining sites would eliminate some of those. We are also aware that there would be some small measure of alleviation from flooding in parts of the county if further reservoirs were built. We would ask you to believe that we have given full weight to these possible advantages.

'It is a source of great anxiety to this Committee that the Consultants who are likely to be engaged in this survey would be asked to give consideration to matters with which they are not qualified to deal. In particular they will be asked to make some very technical decisions about land use, the value of agricultural production and other related matters without, it would appear to us, the necessary expert opinions to make such technical analyses, or to make them credible.

'We know it has been suggested that it is open to this Committee or indeed any other person or body, to make all these objections known at a Public Inquiry, but we feel this would be quite wrong. It should be the responsibility of the Government or any of its chosen instruments to satisfy the nation that all aspects of water supply and usage are being considered and not just this one method of drowning one valley after another.

'This really is the heart of our objections. We would ask now, for the future peace of mind of this entire area, that a clear declaration of the final limit to which these developments will be allowed to go, shall be clearly stated. It is the earnest hope of this Committee that we may have succeeded in going some way towards persuading you of the necessity to do so and to do it as quickly as it can practically be done.'

A reply came from Cledwyn Hughes saying:

'I am very disappointed to learn from your letter of 26 January that despite the explanations and assurances I gave at the recent meeting in Newtown, your Committee has decided that it cannot co-operate in the visual inspection of potential sites. In recent months I have given considerable thought to all the objections that have been raised to a survey of potential reservoir sites on the Severn and have, I think, by limiting the number of sites to be examined and by meeting your Committee, personally done my best to allay fears and anxieties.

'The economic prosperity of England and Wales and the improvement of living standards of large numbers of people require that (at least until desalination or estuarine barrages become economic propositions) the resources of our major rivers should be more fully used. By helping to attract new industries, to improve amenities, to promote tourism and to reduce the risks of flooding, new reservoirs at carefully chosen sites should bring benefits to Mid Wales as well as to other parts of the country. Of course, they are not the complete answer to the need to reduce flooding.'

He went on to give assurances that he would be ready to respond if the Committee changed its mind.

At the next meeting of the Mid Wales (Reservoirs) Defence Committee on 20 February 1967, Gordon Pugh read a prepared statement from the Dulas Valley Defence Committee stating that the original decision of his committee was to agree to survey, but it was not the intention of his local committee to undermine the influence of the Mid Wales Defence Committee. Being vehemently opposed to the desecration of valleys, the Dulas Committee were solidly behind the main Defence Committee in its opposition to the plans of the Authority.

In a letter written to those affected, Mr R. P. Davies, Secretary of the Mid Wales (Reservoirs) Defence Committee, wrote:

'It appears that the test of plans to defend your valleys may now be upon us and those plans will operate as arranged by your local committees.

I am to remind you of your right to object to entry on your land and if entry takes place without your permission that you should ask that person to leave. If he does not leave or refuses to leave you should ask him if he has a Magistrate's warrant to enter, in which case this should be addressed to you by name and read or presented to you. This, however, is most unlikely at this juncture as an application to a Magistrate for a warrant can only follow the giving of notice to you of the intention to seek such a warrant. If no warrant is possessed then you may eject the person using no more force than is necessary to accomplish that task.'

He finished by telling them to act civilly yet resolutely without recourse to arguments, abuse or violence, because such acts could quickly lead to being on the wrong side of the law.

The last minutes of the Mid Wales (Reservoirs) Defence Committee in my possession appear to be those of 5 May 1967 when the Chairman urged patience and a continuing interest in the matter.

Then came the news that we had dreaded. The Severn River Authority had requested the Secretary of State for Wales to make an order under Section 67 of the Water Resources Act 1963 permitting them to carry out trial borings with a view to constructing a dam and regulating reservoir in the Dulas Valley.

On 24 April 1967 Iorwerth Evans, Secretary of the Dulas Valley Defence Committee, received a letter from the Clerk to the Severn River Authority stating:

'You may recall that I wrote to you in March 1966 concerning investigations being carried out by this Authority, in pursuance of its powers and duties under the Water Resources Act, into possible sites for regulating and flood relief reservoirs.

Those investigations are being carried out on behalf of the Authority by Messrs Binnie and Partners,

Consulting Engineers, who will be accompanied by representatives of Messrs Cooke and Arkwright, Land Agents, and will consist initially of a visual survey of the land. The investigations have unfortunately been delayed but it is now hoped to carry them out during the next few weeks, and it may be necessary for the representatives to enter on your land in the Dulas Valley for this purpose.

The survey is being carried out with the agreement of the Secretary of State, who has emphasised the desirability of assessing the potentialities of the sites as soon as possible so as to remove local uncertainties and I trust that the Authority will have your co-operation.'

It was now in black and white and had become a reality. The entire community would have to galvanise its efforts further and move up a few gears. This posed no problem for such a cohesive, determined group of people.

At a meeting of the Dulas Valley Defence Committee on 2 May 1967, as a result of this letter, it was decided not to co-operate with the Severn River Authority for the survey, but to vigorously oppose it. With the support of local people, the Committee would do everything in its power to fight this threat using every conceivable means other than resorting to breaking the law. The Committee unanimously decided to flatly refuse entry onto land.

The bullying attitude of the Authority caused us much concern, as did the apparent indifference of Government. Was there collusion, and were we perhaps becoming the victims of *subversion* prior to *submersion*? Only time would tell.

Chapter Two

The Proposals

Fears grew when it became known that the Severn River Authority not only considered the Dulas Upper and Lower sites to be the most suitable for their requirements, but were seeking to carry out trial borings and detailed inspections. A sombre mood descended like a very low cloud upon the people of the Valley and the whole community was filled with turmoil and despair. We had believed that it could never happen to us. We could not accept that the place we loved, the source of our livelihoods for many generations, was now in jeopardy.

It was gut wrenching news. At first, there was a mood of resignation: was it not an inevitability? My own father said gloomily, 'There is not much we can do, other than register our opposition.' I had been brought up with my seven brothers and sisters in this peaceful and cherished place. We had been nurtured in an atmosphere of love and security, with respect for the land around us and for the people who lived and worked out their lives there. Our parents were deeply rooted in the values and the culture which enfolded us. We were not alone.

We wondered how much longer we could enjoy the many seasonal delights we had cherished – the trees greening in the early spring, the first primrose, the familiar call of curlews, lapwings and a host of other birds. We always greeted eagerly the sound of the cuckoo, heralding the approach of summer. How could we live without the cacophony of new born lambs? And then there was summer itself – the sweet smell of freshly mown hay and long summer evenings when we played our spirited games along the fields and hedgerows. Were we to be denied the annual tapestry of autumn when the woods were streaked in gold and red? What of Christmas and the winter snows? It was not romantic nostalgia – just a genuine, intrinsic love of our way of life. We knew no other.

Slowly, our determination to defeat this iniquitous threat grew. Our close community was not to be robbed of everything it valued. Collectively we drew strength from deep and abiding roots.

No doubt the River Authority thought of the Dulas Valley as just another sparsely populated zone in the barren wasteland they believed Mid Wales to be. They needed to build a dam to provide water for the Midlands and they needed it soon – in fact by 1975. Even the newly appointed Secretary of State for Wales, the Welsh Labour MP George Thomas, seemed prepared to see this scheme go through without thought of its impact upon the people. We saw George Thomas as a renegade who was prepared to sell his country down the river. Like many others, he expressed the opinion that valleys in Wales would have to be sacrificed to meet the growing demand for water in England. Which particular sites the River Authority earmarked seemed of no concern to him. He, a Welshman, was prepared to sacrifice our vibrant community on the altar of political power. Was he not aware that there were adequate supplies of water in other, more accessible parts of the United Kingdom? Did he, or anyone, have the right to destroy our homes and livelihoods, drown our farms and villages and bring our way of life to an end without any attempt to examine alternatives?

We had watched the fate of the people of Fyrnwy, of Elan and Clywedog who had lost their beautiful valleys to the demands of Liverpool and the Midlands. Mostly they had neither been consulted nor considered. At Fyrnwy, not a single Welsh planning officer, engineer or consultant had been involved at any stage.

The loss of Tryweryn to the north of us was the most emotive. To this day, the very mention of the name arouses passion in the hearts of Welsh people. The entire village of Capel Celyn and its surrounding farms were drowned to provide water for the city of Liverpool. That in itself was hugely traumatic, but the manner in which the scheme was accomplished was insensitive, draconian and totally heedless of the impact on the Welsh speaking community, its chapel and graveyard and its distinctive culture. The imperious officials were seen as Philistines. In advertising the scheme, they failed to mention even that Capel Celyn was in Wales. The water engineer was from Liverpool, the consulting engineers were London based, the contractors who built the dam came from Wolverhampton, and the so-called fishery adviser from Aberdeen. The landscape consultant, charged with the sensitive task of blending this artificial lake into the surrounding hills, was not a Jones, an Evans or a Davies, but Sir Frederick Gibberd, architect of Liverpool Cathedral, who had gained his reputation in building new towns in England.

Sympathy for the people of Capel Celyn grew rapidly in Wales. The provocation was so great that retaliation was inevitable – in February 1963, a power transformer was blown up by protesters and, later, an electricity pylon. It sparked further direct action in other parts of Wales. People went to jail. Thankfully, we have moved on, but

Tryweryn will *never* be forgotten or forgiven. Forty years later, Liverpool formally apologised for what had happened.

Our torment began just as the Tryweryn project was nearing its completion. The Tryweryn dam had been built on the site of *Tyddyn Halt* on the Trawsfynydd to Bala railway line. Was it a coincidence that the proposed Dulas dam was to be built very near the site of *Tylwch Halt* on the Brecon to Moat Lane line? The locations and particularly the names seemed too similar. This was another example of how 'the powers that be' appeared to be conspiring against us. That was probably a figment of our imagination, but had the effect of strengthening our resolve. We were simply not going to give in to the demands of a giant Authority. We owed it to those who had lost their hearth and home in other valleys to fight on. We were not going to surrender: insurrection was the only way forward. But our strategy was not violence: it had failed at Tryweryn. We would lock horns with the proposers in a different way. Perhaps we should adopt Bulwer-Lytton's maxim – 'the pen is mightier than the sword'. Ideas started to be put on paper and our strategy and tactics began to emerge.

The Water Authorities were powerful forces, seemingly too big to oppose. At the beginning we had no idea where to start fighting the leviathan of Severn-Trent. We were innocent country folk who lived peaceful yet busy lives in a beautiful part of mid Wales. We farmed in the week. We attended our chapels on Sunday. Young people who did not leave for college or university, found employment locally and there were lively Young Farmers' Clubs and Young Peoples' Guilds to enhance their social lives. We troubled no one, helped out in our community and kept ourselves to ourselves, upholding the values which had been passed

Welsh farmers fight water war

Farmers of the Dulas Valley in Central Wales are at war.

Who are they fighting?

The farmers' enemy is the Severn Water Board. The Board plans to flood 1,400 acres of the Dulas Valley to make a new reservoir.

At one end of the Dulas Valley there are steep mountains. At the other end there are gentle slopes of good grazing land.

Most of the people who live in the Valley are farming families.

of Wales provide water fo cities which are often mile

Beauty spot t be submerged

A valley described recently as an outstandingly beautiful spot may be submerged to create another regulating reservoir in Montgomeryshire.

The Severn River Authority announced yesterday that their water resources committee were recommending an immediate detailed investigation of the lower Dulas Valley site, in South

and fifteen will be partly submerged, and the hamlet of Tylwch with its eight houses will also go under.

the committee wo on Wdnesday to this new developme The valley is serv parish church, tw

Thomas plumps *feb 19* for the reservoir

by Robin Oakley

WELSH Secretary of State Mr George Thomas day warned that, despite advances in water vation techniques, it was unlikely that any tive to the building of large reservoirs would in the next few years.

He told the Council of the Institution of Water Engineers in London that this did not mean he believed that reservoirs could be established regardless of social amenity considerations.

He looked with hope to the possibility of obtaining water through the process of desalination but a major study published by the Water Resources Board has shown this was unlikely to be an economic proposition within the next thirty years.

down from previous generations. Life was good and we were going to do our utmost to preserve what we had.

The community began to galvanise itself into a great collective effort. We had carefully to orchestrate a strategy which would achieve our objectives. We had to take positive steps to get the show on the road. We began by collecting together a list of the homes and holdings which would be lost under the proposed reservoir. We saw it as a necessary if onerous task, but as the extent of the destruction was borne in upon us, it was very sobering. For a start, we would lose the picturesque but essential link, the B4518, between Llanidloes and Rhayader. It would be wiped off the map. The Valley was steep and precipitous where it narrowed at the site of the proposed dam. How on earth could a replacement road be built without a huge diversion? What thought had been given to that?

The proposed reservoir was to stretch for nearly four miles, commencing just north of the village of Tylwch and finishing on the outskirts of Pantydwr. Four small tributary valleys would also be under water. Twenty-five properties would be lost altogether, including complete farms. Fifty farms would lose some land and 1,400 acres of good, farmed agricultural land would be submerged. The reservoir was to hold 18 billion gallons of water, would take in excess of three years to fill and would cost around £11 million – a much more significant figure in those days than even now.

At its most northerly point, the reservoir was to have begun just above Tylwch, straddling the old railway line on land belonging to Cwmfron on the one side and Penybanc on the other. Penybanc House and the beautiful little hamlet of Tylwch would be submerged, encompassing 1, 2 and 3 Rock Cottages and Pen Caer Driw house with its well-maintained garden and croquet lawn. Station House and the former railway station would disappear under the water, along with The Cottage, Brook Cottage and Hill View. The reservoir would spread up the Waen Cilgwyn Valley as far as Ty'nllidiart, and affect Tyndderw, Cefn, Hendreaur Chapel and the borders of Dol-y-gors. Oleddu Isaf, Oleddu Uchaf and White Gate. It would also affect Railway Cottage, the Old Parsonage, Pen-y-Graig, Plas Tylwch, West Fedw and Lower Fedw.

The Llydiartywaen Valley would not escape. Land belonging to The Park, Old Chapel, Llwydiarth, Tyddynycwm, Birches, Bryhesglyn, Garth Fawr and Clydfanau would be inundated.

The farmhouses which would be totally submerged were Glanyrafon, Brynhir, Cenarth Mill, Llwynbenglog, Fullbrook, Rhosfelin, Rhosgoch Fawr, Rhosgoch Fach and Cnych Fach. Sychnant Fawr, Sychnant Fach, Babylon, Tanycoed, Croesty, Alltllwyd, Llidiarddau, Penddol, Eisteddlle, Nantgwyn, Llwybrain, Bryncenarth and Pwll would be affected to a lesser degree.

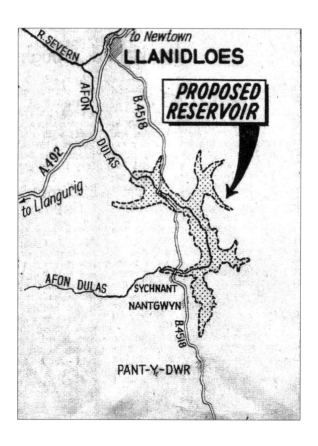

My father drew up his own handwritten list which also showed the peripheral farms which were likely to lose a small portion of land: Tynllidiart, Hirfron, Cwmdulas, Pantydwgan and Stores Farm.

The life and livelihoods of the Dulas Valley were threatened with obliteration.

Chapter Three

The Fightback Begins

In the spring of 1968, there began a flurry of telephone calls, discussions and lengthy interviews with press and television. The Dulas Valley Defence Committee started to plan our response in earnest. A meeting was fixed for the 8th of May by my father, Iorwerth Evans, and Gordon Pugh. Invitations to attend were sent to both the Secretary and the Chairman of the Mid Wales (Reservoirs) Defence

Iorwerth Evans (Chair), R. P. Davies, Gordon Pugh (Secretary), John Price (Treasurer) and Leslie Morgan

Committee, R. P. Davies of the Farmers Union of Wales and Leslie Morgan. I was asked by my father to take notes of the meeting. Everyone who attended was nervous and anxious, not knowing what precisely had happened up to this point in time, let alone what was looming up on the horizon. My father chaired the proceedings.

Mr Morgan opened the discussion, telling us that he and Mr Davies had thought that they should first find out the opinion of the people involved before calling a meeting of the main Defence Committee – which, of course, was concerned with all possible sites in Mid Wales. He said that whatever action we might decide upon, we would have the support of the main Committee. They had read the Report of the Water Resources Board prepared for the Severn River Authority. He pointed out that the Authority was nothing more than the servant of the WRB, who were insisting that the SRA had to get more water by the 1970s. In answer to a question, he stated that the SRA had not said why our valley had been chosen. The proposal had been that they investigate all possible sites, and the Secretary of State had asked the SRA to review them all.

In an intervention, Mr Bound of Llwynbrain expressed his surprise that this site had been fixed upon at all. He hoped that the authorities concerned were aware that this was a stock-raising area, producing some of the best stock that went to local markets. Some of the land was not very good, but the best parts were at the riverside where cattle could find shade and water. Still, there would be plenty of water, if the scheme went through! People who had left the hills to go down country had done so out of choice and the people of Dulas Valley owed no duty to them to supply them with water. He complained that we had not known much about what was going on – only hearing in the last year or two.

The Reverend T. J. Williams of the Manse asked whether it was possible to make a dam in the Lower Dulas which would leave the Upper Dulas alone. But it appeared that even if the Lower Dulas were developed, both sites would be affected. Mr Watkins of Llidiardau and Mr Emrys Evans of Green Farm made it clear that the main business of the meeting was to defend the Valley and stop the building of any dam anywhere. My father asked whether there was anyone who was prepared to sell his land to the SRA; prepared to be a quisling and stick a knife in the back of the majority. Mr Evans proposed that they all held firmly together: he called for a show of hands to find out whether there was anyone prepared to make a private deal and act as turncoats. No one raised their hand.

Mr Morgan of the Defence Committee urged a vote – it would be extremely valuable for our future case if it was unanimous. A vote was then taken demonstrating complete opposition to any further move forward by the SRA.

Mr Morgan then outlined what was likely to happen. Each person affected would receive a letter stating that the Authority wished to enter their land. The Surveyor would arrive and he should be told that entry was refused. After such a refusal, he would seek to arrive at the gate with a police sergeant. But, he advised, every step should be taken to delay that awful day when a Court Warrant would be issued. We should not weaken our resolve but exercise patience – delay would be to our advantage, not disadvantage. We should say that we did not know the size or height of the dam or any other important details. Each individually should immediately contact the NFU or FUW County Secretary and tell him that as members of his union, on the information we had been given, we were not prepared to co-operate with the SRA. The County

Secretaries should then inform the SRA that their members were in full accord with the letter which the Defence Committee would be sending. The Reverend Williams was anxious that the Members of Parliament for both constituencies should also be contacted.

So the fight back began. The SRA responded by offering to meet with the people who lived in the Valley and a further meeting was called for the 27th of May to discuss their response. Mr Morgan outlined the history. It was in February 1966 when the SRA first requested the farming unions and local authorities in Montgomeryshire to attend a meeting in Newtown to explain its proposals concerning a survey of the Upper Severn basin. At the time there was no great public concern, but when maps and a list of people affected was produced some weeks later it became apparent that a very large portion of Montgomeryshire would be under water. There were twenty-nine separate dam sites involved. This led to the formation of the Mid Wales (Reservoirs) Defence Committee. That committee was now prepared to follow whatever lead the Dulas Committee wished to take. The SRA had reduced their proposals to this one site only, but that would not be the end of it. The proposed Dulas dam would only meet their requirements for five years and the SRA could be coming back with a new proposal every year without ever attempting to find any other source of water.

Mr Morgan assured the meeting that the other twenty-eight named sites would not be sitting back with relief and the Mid Wales Defence Committee would give us enthusiastic support for action against the proposals.

As for the size of the proposed reservoir, Mr Watson of the Country Landowners Association told the meeting that he had received a letter which stated that the water line would be at the 935-feet contour line. There was discussion about an approach to the new Secretary of State for Wales, George Thomas, and a desire to keep Cledwyn Hughes, his predecessor, to his promise that no more communities in Wales would be drowned. Mr Powell of Fullbrook proposed that all should go to the meeting with the SRA in the Community Centre in Llanidloes in the following week and it was agreed that Mr Leslie Morgan should act as the chief spokesman not only for the Mid Wales Defence Committee but for our valley as well. Mr Morgan was anxious that in addition to any opening statement he might make, as many people as possible who were affected should have their direct say. As Mr Emrys Evans put it, 'This is the first time that we have come out into the open.' My father and the Reverend Williams were anxious that the question of compensation should not be raised by anyone. My father said, 'They should realise that we are in a fight which is a matter of life and death.'

It was also agreed that they should not, for this first meeting, seek to involve any supporters from outside. John Tudor, who had been a member of the Committee opposing the Clywedog project, said about local authority involvement, 'We found in Clywedog that there was nothing being done. I suggest that you decide here and now what you want done and then call the local authorities in to help you – we found them very useful when we asked them for help.' Committee member Mr Emrys Evans, a Radnorshire County Councillor, and representatives of other local authorities gave their support, but the overall feeling was that in the initial stages, it was up to us. Letters were nevertheless to be sent to the County Councils, the Rural District Councils and Parish Councils who would be affected. The NFU, represented by Mr R. V. Morgan, gave us full support.

Mr Leslie Morgan roused the meeting with his final

words: 'All that we can do is to make it clear to them that they are not going to have a walkover. Get up and say that your homes and your farms are going to be drowned, and you will not have it. Let them understand the nature of the opposition they are likely to run into.'

The workload was obviously too much for one man with a farming business to run and it was proposed that Gordon Pugh should remain the local contact but that his burden should be taken up by Mr R. P. Davies, a full-time official of the FUW.

It was an exceptional meeting but we continued to spend months living with the thought that our days in the Valley were numbered, and with the uncertainty that dragged on. Was it worth carrying on with farm improvements, new intensive methods of farming, when one day all would be taken away? And what we could not understand was that a planning application for building a caravan site and country club in the Valley had shortly before been refused on the grounds that it was an area 'of outstanding natural beauty.' What had changed?

By now, we had won the backing of the NFU, the FUW, Radnorshire County Council, Newtown, Llanidloes and Rhayader District Councils, the Council for the Protection of Rural Wales, and every branch of the Country Landowners Association in Mid and North Wales. The Presbyterian Church of Wales and the Baptist Union of Wales were behind us, as was the Federation of Young Farmers' Clubs.

Montgomeryshire County Council were more cautious. At first, they decided to go along with the River Authority and not to back our cause. My father was scathing: 'It is time the Council came off the fence and made a decision. If the Defence Committee had been as inactive as the County Council, the Valley would have been under water by now.' Eventually, by the narrowest of margins, the County Council decided to back our Committee and oppose the scheme. But a vote on whether or not to attend at the Public Inquiry and hold a watching brief was defeated by a single vote. We had our supporters amongst the councillors. One said the SRA had not substantiated its case. Another said, 'There's a lot of good land in the Dulas Valley – well worked by jolly good farmers.' One excuse given for inaction was that the information they required had been refused. The Council were told by the SRA that if it was not the Dulas, then two other valleys in the county would have to be considered. 'Blackmail!' declared a supportive councillor. 'We must resist this kind of thing.'

MONTGOMERYSHIRE NOW OPPOSED TO DULAS VALLEY FLOOD SCHEME

Montgomeryshire County Council has at last come into line with Radnorshire County Council and Rhayader Rural District Council in deciding to oppose the scheme to flood the Dulas Valley on the borders of the two counties.

Newtown—Llanidloes Rural District Council has also come out in opposition. But the Montgomeryshire decision "that the Severn River Authority had not substantiated a case for investigating the Dulas and that the flooding of the valley be opposed" was carried at a special meeting of the County Council at Welshpool on Monday.

Many people not only from Montgomeryshire and Radnorshire but from other parts of the country expressed their willingness and readiness to come to our valley and give their help. It had become an issue of national importance. We were fighting not just for our own homes and livelihoods, but for the other valleys in Mid Wales

Brynhir – a farm right in the middle of the affected area.

Cenarth Mill – my birthplace and childhood home that would have been totally submerged.

*The bridge over the River Dulas that as a child
I was afraid of crossing.*

*Pencaedriw, the home of Col & Mrs Hough, whose tree planting
greatly enhanced the valley.*

High above Tylwch, only the chimneys of Penybanc Farm would have been above water level.

Tylwch Halt as it is today, with only an old railway van giving away its former life.

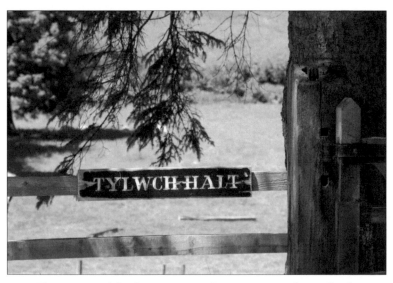

The owners of the former station house are proud to call it by the original name.

The scenic beauty of the valley is there for all to see.

*The dam would have crossed the valley at roughly this point just
to the north of Tylwch.*

*The River Dulas near to where the dam would have loomed
large, on its way to meet the Severn just west of Llanidloes.*

A panoramic view looking eastwards from above Tylwch and down the old Brecon to Moat Lane railway line. Rhydd Hywel hill, after which our YFC Choir was named, can be seen in the distance.

Evidence of balanced, sustainable land use – well farmed fields, adjacent areas set aside for wildlife... and vistas that are pleasing to the eye. What more can one ask for?

Cheerful Brick Cottage, lighting up the scene, would have found itself at the very bottom of the reservoir. Low flying Fighter Pilots would have missed seeing this notable landmark during their training sorties.

Evening shadows fall. They have nothing on the shadow that might have befallen this bewitching landscape, had the planners had their way.

A hazy spring day at Lower Fedw, typifying the Dulas Valley at its very best.

Baptisms still take place in this deceptively deep pool on the Dulas near Rhyd Meheryn (Rams Ford) just south of Glanyrafon Farm.

A spur of the reservoir would have extended westwards along Waun Cilgwyn. This valley with its rolling landscape has a beauty all of its own, the loss of which would have been tragic.

Tens of thousands of daffodils line the B4518 road for over a mile just south of Tylwch, a sight appreciated each spring by both locals and tourists alike. This was, and still is, a community that very much cares for its environment. What, I wonder, would William Wordsworth have made of such a host?

Grade II listed Sychnant Presbyterian Chapel, built in 1825, still opens its doors every Sunday. It was where my husband and I were married. During summer, tea has for generations been served between afternoon and evening services – a long held tradition.

Penddol – an old Welsh longhouse and home to our much loved 'Uncle Fred'. Family ties are so important in remote rural areas.

Nantgwyn Primary School once echoed to the joyous sounds of young children, ourselves included. Sadly, like many others, it is now a private residence, but at least is in use.

The valley is renowned for the quality of stock it turns out. Note also the tidily trimmed hedge – evidence if needed of pride in the way the land is farmed generally.

The substantial prominence of Nantgwyn Baptist Chapel, where the service of thanksgiving was held following the celebration of our victory.

The lane leading to Bryncenarth – my mother's home. Behind it is Cefncenarth Hill, the unchanged outline of which would undoubtedly have been very familiar to Owain Glyndŵr whilst visiting his daughter and son-in-law Philip ap Rhys.

Pantydwr village, seen here from near Garth Farm (home of Gordon Pugh), a site on the southern fringe of the proposed reservoir.

The northern edge of Pantydwr village at Rhosforgan. The water level would have reached just beyond the road sign.

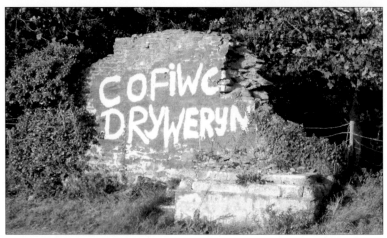

Many readers will doubtless be familiar with the 'Cofiwch Tryweryn' mural and its history, as shown and described on Page 14.

The colour photographs shown here illustrate the ongoing refurbishment of this icon of Welsh nationhood. The first shows it in a former weather worn guise, while the second is as it appeared during late 2018, looking very spruce, signifying the poignancy and reverence in which it is held.

Moves are at foot to secure official protection for the mural by The Welsh Assembly Government, given that it means so much to so many of our citizens who are justifiably proud of their heritage.

Residents of the Dulas valley, having witnessed past transgressions, can be proud to have saved their valley due to having been greatly influenced by 'The Tryweryn factor', as reflected in the title of this book.

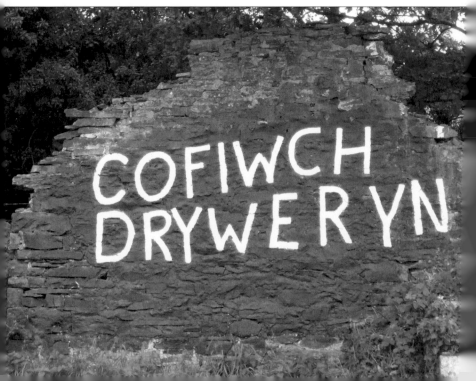

earmarked as future targets. We were determined that Dulas would not become a precedent. A victory for us should not permit the River Authority to pursue its intentions elsewhere. Our determination was getting stronger by the day – but then came a bombshell.

In the autumn of 1968, we were alarmed to see contractors working upstream from Tylwch. A similar construction had been built in Clywedog before work on the dam there had begun. Buttingtons of Welshpool, the contractors, said they were building a 'Gauging Station' in preparation for the main contract for the scheme. 'Not at all,' said a spokesman for the SRA: they were merely building a river flow measuring station which was not directly connected with the proposals for the dam – it would however be an important feature if the reservoir were built. But it was 'just a gauge for measuring the flow of water in the Dulas at different times of the year.' They said there were similar installations on other rivers in the area and it would have been built regardless of the dam construction.

Did they really think we were that naïve? Gullibility was never a characteristic of the hard working and surprisingly canny, intuitive folk of our valley. We had no intention of being duped.

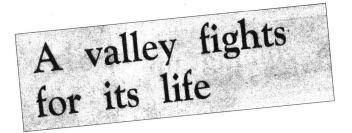

Spare this land for agriculture

by DAVID LLOYD

Once again those concerned with providing water to slake the unquenchable thirst of Britain's expanding urban areas have triggered off anger and anxiety in a peaceful Welsh Valley.

Year by year the demand for water and ___ bound to inc___ to___ pr___

boundary near Llanidloes and another on the Usk near Sennybridge, Breconshire.

This week I visited the Dulas Valley in Montgomeryshire and Radnorshire to see the valley that has been given the kiss of death following ___ouncement that the ___Authority

intentions. That they sh be consulted.

The benefits that w accrue to urban areas tourist and recreati interests were all claimed. But no reassur about the disruption w the Dulas Valley.

To make matters w maps received by far and others indicated

CHARLES CHEER SAD VALLEY

LEADERS of a campaign to save a Welsh valley from being submerged for a new reservoir have found a new ally — Prince Charles.

For in a speech last week the Prince hit out at "the tragic business of reservoir construction."

He said it increased the urgency of a plan to get drinking water from

enormous at first," Prince Charles said at Cardiff, "but surely worth it long-term."

His comments came a week before a public inquiry opens—on Tuesday —into a scheme which is the most controversial issue in the principality.

reservoir in the Dulas Valley in mid-Wales. It would disrupt the lives of 150 people and engulf 1,400 acres of farmland.

Water

Yesterday farm___ Iorwerth E___ man

he was "bucked" Prince's remarks Mr. Evans ad___ have always s should get water flooding valleys.

"What Prince has said may authorities a littl make them realise not alone. And Conservation Wales ___

THE BRITISH

SOCIETY SHOULD NOT BE DESTROYED

___uld have thought you ___get a matter of absorb-___ from two documents ___osaic titles? Let no one ___however, by an investi-___bears the somewhat off-___cription: "A survey of ___c and Community ___cs" nor, from a Local ___Chronicle, an article by ___yer on Reservoirs ___. Both are necessary to ___picture of what is pro-___ Dulas Valley near by ___nd Rhayader in central

___always calculated to ___hot controversy in the

an order permitting them to carry out trial borings with a view to constructing a dam and regulating reservoir in the Dulas Valley. The case of more than local interest because large issues are involved. In particular there is the all-important consideration in what proportion you must weigh the economic and sociological factors. There can be no doubt that after possible sites had been reduced to ten in number, two sites in the Dulas Valley were recommended by the consultants for trial borings. They obviously did so because they felt that this area was most suitable for their purpose. Nevertheless it seems obvious that they did not conduct ___ sort of preliminary sociological

which the community was engaged This they illustrated by a number of figures which tellingly reinforce their points. The tables, in fact, are a most valuable part of the survey. Their conclusion was quite unambiguous. They acknowledged that here, as elsewhere in the upland areas of mid-Wales, the population is decreasing. Nevertheless, it is not any more advanced in this region. They were not aware of any evidence which could be adduced to suggest that farming was precarious. Speak___

might appear to be empty and to have no central point, yet the rich-ness of its community linkages might be far greater than those in modern suburbia. One must never under-estimate these community links just because they cannot be evaluated in cost/benefit terms.

They make good use of Alwyn Rees's passage from a work of Alwyn Rees: The failure of the urban world to give its inhabitants status and signi-ficance in a functioning society, and their consequent disintegration into

matter when the Public Enquiry was set up. He also felt that the pro-posed flooding of the Dulas sites had not taken into account the socio-logical factors and that these were of major importance. He believes that the 300 people in the valley are not only a real and identifiable community but that the agriculture is capable of supporting them. He comes to the conclusion, on the evidence produced, that this is an ex-tremely talented and thriving com-munity. He gives high marks to th___

Chapter Four

Views and Opinions

The story of our valley and our resistance to the plans of the Severn River Authority became news country-wide. We were swamped with reporters and commentators from national newspapers. Our plight was featured not just on Welsh regional television, but also on national channels. *Women's Hour* took it up, as did the BBC1 programme *24 hours* under the banner of *The Great Water Rush* during which the Rhydd Hywel Youth Choir performed.

Familiar television presenters came to interview us – Trevor Fishlock, Julian Pettifer, and David Richardson of the BBC *Farming* programme.

Prince Charles showed his concern for the countryside and hit out about '. . . the tragic business of reservoir construction.' He declared that it increased the urgency of developing desalination plants to source drinking water from the sea. The cost might be enormous at first, but surely it was worth it in the long term.

The Severn River Authority responded, pointing out the advantages they believed would come for tourism and recreation and the benefits to local towns. A spokesman said that the need was fairly urgent, proclaiming that the Authority had chosen a site for the new reservoir which, as well as being ideal, would disturb the least number of people possible. Research into barrage schemes was ongoing but the Dulas Valley scheme was essential despite the understandable opposition of those whom he dubbed '*The Welsh*'. We found this slighting reference to us Welsh people as demeaning to say the least. It evoked further memories of Tryweryn. Our community, having welcomed incomers in the past, had shown neither nationalistic nor xenophobic tendencies.

We now began to wonder whether subjugation had ever been consigned to the history books. Was the spirit of Edward I still alive? It certainly did appear so. Surely there were vast tracts of far more sparsely populated hill country in the north east of England which were eminently suitable, and which would cause far less disruption to communities. Clearly, the Dulas Valley was disadvantaged by its proximity to the Midlands and the precedents afforded by the annexation of Clywedog, Elan, Fyrnwy and Tryweryn. Doubtless at the end of the day, fiscal consideration would be paramount over the needs and rights of small communities to live their lives as they always had done. Money talks. For a moment, it seemed that the death of our valley was inevitable.

Edward Millward, then the prospective Plaid Cymru candidate for Montgomeryshire and later Prince Charles' tutor in the Welsh language, spoke up for us. He said that Tryweryn was a turning point in the history of the development of Welsh water resources for outside use. Although public opinion in Wales was united in its opposition and in spite of the fact that a majority of Welsh MPs had voted against Tryweryn, the scheme had been forced upon an unwilling populace. The weight of united Welsh opinion against the Tryweryn project merely served to emphasise the utter helplessness of Welsh people and their Parliamentary representatives in such matters. He

continued that no unequivocal leadership or defence would
come from Whitehall, but if the people of the Dulas Valley
believed in themselves, nothing could stand in their way.

David Lloyd of the *Liverpool Daily Post* wrote
sympathetically:
> 'In many respects the lower reaches of the Valley would
> appear to be a dam designer's dream come true, with a
> narrow valley enclosed by two natural rock buttresses
> only a few hundred yards apart. Upstream, however, the
> Valley opens out into as fine a livestock rearing plateau
> as one might find anywhere in Wales. In certain
> respects, the land is as good as many a lowland plain
> except that it means that spring comes a little later and
> the grazing season is too short for economic
> production. But in terms of beef, lamb, seed potatoes
> and cereals for home feed, the Valley sets a high
> standard in terms of productive potential. It is the sort
> of land Wales can ill afford to lose. Not only would a
> number of farms be submerged, but many more would
> be seriously unbalanced if they lost the bottom land and
> were left with only the upper slopes. One farmer came
> up with a fitting analogy – "It would be like asking a
> manufacturer to give up his production line, but
> allowing him to keep the warehouse." '

Samuel Knight of the *Western Mail* wrote:
> 'Most of the homes in the Valley have mains electricity
> and piped water supply, and the bulk of the houses are
> well equipped by contemporary standards.
> Spearheading the Dulas Valley Defence Committee is
> Mr Iorwerth Evans, who faces the prospect of losing his
> home and best farming land. He is a tenant farmer and
> likely to be among the worst affected. As a tenant his

compensation would be limited to five times his annual rent, plus an allowance for disturbance.'

Mary Holland, assisted by Joanna Slater of the *Observer*, gave us a full column. They wrote:

'Spring comes a little late to Dulas, but apart from that, the Valley bears comparison with cattle breeding far to the south. The quality of the soil has been changed by generations of good husbandry. The men and women who live here form a passionately-rooted community, their lives built around the traditions of their religion and their farms. Gordon Pugh's family left good farming land to come here in the seventeenth Century to escape the religious persecution of nonconforming sects in England and to build its chapels and practice their faith in freedom. It was people like this, hardworking, God fearing, Bible reading, who changed the land. Mr Pugh now runs a large farm by modern methods . . .

'. . . Iorwerth Evans, spry and eloquent, is a tenant farmer in his sixties with a connoisseur's ear for a good phrase, his own and that of other people. He has eight children and a bonny wife. The whole family go around Wales, singing and reciting from the great tradition nurtured by the chapels. The dresser in their kitchen is overflowing with silver cups won at Eisteddfodau over the years. It seems that the singing out of the Dulas may have to stop.'

Another newspaper reported that the proposed reservoir would undoubtedly flood a very beautiful hamlet, some lovely countryside and productive farmland.

'The standard of farming in the community is high and the quality of the stock produced is remarkable. The

farmers take great pride in their work and it shows.
Now all this is threatened and determination is written
all over their faces. They are not going to take this lying
down. What right does anyone have to come along and
take away the very ground on which they stand and
where they make a living?'

Inevitably, there were a few who thought it was a good idea
to flood the Valley. Perhaps they thought they were
protecting their own patch. E. S. Jenkins of Llanidloes, a
staunch supporter of the then Labour government, wrote
jointly with Mervyn Jones to the *County Times* on 1
February 1969 under the startling heading: *Most people are
in favour of Dulas plan*. They thought too much publicity
had been given to the critics of the scheme and it was
about time other points of view were presented:

'Let us look at some of the facts. About sixty properties
are involved if the Dulas dam is built. Some people will
lose their homes, a few will lose all their land, and
others a few acres. ALL will be compensated. We agree
that the hardest hit will be the tenant farmers, and it
would be fair if these were to receive special
compensation. Land and property owners will receive
adequate payment, and if Clywedog is anything to go
by, the majority will be crying all the way to the bank.

'If our MP's proposals are to be taken seriously, it
means that more good agricultural land will be taken to
build his proposed trunk road through to Aberystwyth
than will be flooded by the Dulas dam.

'Now let us present some benefits of the scheme.
There must be hundreds of people in Montgomeryshire
alone who suffer great hardship every year because of
flooding caused by the Severn bursting its banks. The
inhabitants of Caersws, Newtown and Llandrinio – and

these are Welsh too – must be very relieved by the extent the Clywedog Dam has helped the flood problem and another dam on the Severn or the Dulas would practically eliminate the danger.

'Three to four hundred men drawn from all parts of the county and part of Radnorshire would enjoy five years of well paid work, the traders five years of prosperity and there would be permanent staff needed afterwards. The tourist trade would get another boost – and we must say we cannot understand the apathy of Llanidloes Chamber of Trade.

'Why do they remain silent when there is so much they could do to offset the arguments of a minority who are against this scheme and who are for the most part outsiders anyway? We are positive that the majority of working class people in Montgomeryshire are in favour – so please do not let the minority have all the publicity and, Llanidloes Chamber of trade . . . wake up!'

Cynric Mytton-Davies, a local reporter, was hardly a friend of the Dulas Valley inhabitants either. He would have been quite happy to have seen the plans go ahead and had ideas of increasing the flooding potential considerably by including Marteg and Marcheini Valleys between St Harmon and Marteg. He could envisage an increase in tourism. He could see how both Llanidloes and Rhayader would benefit greatly from a 'Welsh Lake District' development if more hotels, guest houses and shops were built. In fact, he fantasised over new shops selling jewellery, fine glass, china and ladies wear. Such whimsical ideology seemed totally misplaced in the order of things. What, we wondered, was his motive? In fact, although we found his attitude heartless, daunting us considerably, it only served to strengthen our resolve.

It has to be admitted that one or two pensioners were willing to accept compensation. They believed that the village of Tylwch was too isolated from nearby towns. There was a bus service four times a day but they thought that would stop soon as few used it. 'Food has to be brought in' they said.

Mrs Elsie Hughes considered that the eighty-member local Defence Committee and the meetings they had held to plan their objections were a waste of time. She had lived in the village for eight years and believed that people who need water should be allowed to have it, even at the expense of Welsh communities. 'We have much more to lose, as we own our homes, than most of those who are fighting for the plans' she said. 'They are mainly tenant farmers anyway.'

A couple who had retired to Tylwch ten years previously said they hoped the Valley would get drowned. 'We have to carry everything here - milk and food. What good will living here be when the buses stop?'

Another resident, a Mr Price, was against any form of violence which, he said, was being suggested by some people, and he must have been a little sceptical when he warned, 'They are talking of trouble, but they fought at Clywedog and that did no good.'

A small number of people in Llanidloes and Rhayader also believed that we were fighting just in order to gain the maximum compensation. This suggestion saddened us somewhat as this was absolutely not the case. When there is the threat of losing one's home and livelihood, then fighting for that is the main priority and the question of compensation comes very much second place. On the other hand, if it became apparent that we were definitely going to lose our fight, then of course it would have been quite a different matter.

Mr R. P. Davies, Secretary of the Defence Committees, commented, 'It would be a miracle if everyone agreed on this. The Severn River Authority themselves are not one hundred per cent in support of drowning the Dulas Valley, and their consultants are equally divided.'

The outstanding journalist Simon Hoggart, wrote in the *Guardian*:

'The Dulas, in Montgomery, is about four miles of rich farming land lying folded into a series of gentle hills, studded with light stone farmhouses. You can hear the trickle of the Dulas, nine hundred feet up from the floor of the Valley, at just about the point where the Severn River Authority proposes to bring its reservoir. If you stand in the garden of William Hough's house (Pencaerdriw, above Tylwch) you can see a whole community living and working beneath you, and picture it entirely drowned by a reservoir almost as deep as Loch Ness.'

He went on to quote Iorwerth Evans, who reflected on the number of Christmases that his family might be able to spend in their Valley home. 'We enjoy life here, we really have a good time,' had said a pensive Mr Evans:

'In his enjoyment there is the life and spirit of a live, flourishing, youthful valley and community. More so than the beauty, more even than the prosperity of the land, it is the death of this sheer enjoyment that will hurt.'

By now we had become inured to the sight of press reporters in the Valley as well as camera crews. They interviewed a number of residents:

Sid Watkins, a fifty-two-year-old farmer told them, 'I will be ruined.' When he moved to his two hundred and twenty acre farm at Llidiarddau in 1952, he had thirty-five cattle and one hundred ewes, but he had increased his stock to one hundred cattle and three hundred and fifty ewes.

'If they flooded the Valley they would take fifty acres of my lowland, and I would be left with only exposed high ground. There would be no winter cover for my cattle, so I would have to reduce my herd. My cattle land would go, making the farm uneconomical.'

Colonel William Hough, a retired army colonel and a veteran of two world wars had lived at Pencaerdriw since 1931. Each year he and his wife had opened their beautiful gardens to raise money for charity. Visitors from all over the county attended to enjoy the magnificent show of rhododendrons and amazing views down the Valley. He was a member of Newtown and Llanidloes Rural District Council. His home would have been one hundred feet under water. He told the reporters:

'The English authorities have been lamentably unimaginative in their quest for water. They're plundering Wales like conquerors. My sorrow about this is not the loss of my home, but a lifetime's work would be destroyed. When I first came here the house was surrounded by fields. Now there are hundreds of rhododendrons – more than forty varieties and I have planted every tree and shrub personally. I hope the local County Councils will back us at the enquiry, then perhaps the River Authority would have to take a look at the proper alternatives such as estuary barrages, instead of using this area for one reservoir scheme after another.'

Gordon Pugh commented that the people in the Dulas Valley were living under a cloud of suspense and blight because of the proposals.

'The last four years have caused a lot of heartache and

mental strain. If a reservoir was ever built, it would cause so much upheaval in the area that it could lead to the mass migration of up to three hundred inhabitants. Many people would be denied the right to live and work in a way that benefited the country and gave them contentment and satisfaction.'

Farming more than eight hundred acres, Mr Pugh claimed:

'I will lose about a hundred and seventy acres if the scheme is approved. Some of my best land – and some poor – will be lost, but my house will remain intact. I will not be as badly off as those farmers who would lose all their lowland shelter area. This valley is one of the best livestock areas in Wales – ask any auctioneer. But most of us are only just viable at the present time. If farmers lost even part of their better land they won't be able to continue. When we were first told a Public Inquiry would take place we asked the Secretary of State for Wales, Mr George Thomas, for financial help to prepare our case, but he replied he had no powers to allocate money in this way. If we had been criminals we would have been granted legal aid; but because we are fighting for our homes, our livelihood and our children, we get no help. That's not justice.'

Ned Price, Brynhir, had two hundred and ten acres of land, one hundred beef cattle and six hundred sheep. His farm would be submerged but for a few acres of hill land: 'I've ordered a new cattle shed – I wonder if it's worth building it now. They will be taking some good farmland if they build this dam.'

Some interviewees were somewhat more belligerent. Take for instance the response from John Price . . . 'Any Englishman asking about water here will get bloody well shot and that's that!'

Mrs Enid Price of The Cottage and her two sisters Mrs Francis Morris and Miss Margaret Powell had spent all their lives in Tylwch.

'Deep down we realised something would happen. The only thing that can save the Valley is if they find the rock strata unsuitable. Some people whose homes were drowned, like those from Clywedog, say that they are better off these days. But you can't be better off if a whole community is lost.'

That last sentence said it all and might well have been pivotal in the minds of the indifferent minority.

David Francis, fifty-two, had worked for thirty-four years as a farm labourer before he inherited the family farm. He would be left with only forty acres. He would lose twenty acres where he made hay every year, four acres where he grew corn and the three acres where he grew swedes for the sheep. He would lose all his farm, Glanyrafon, which he took over from his father. He said:

'This last twelve months we have not known what would happen, but it came as a bit of a shock to hear they were starting site investigations. I can't change from farming now. If I go down country to buy a farm it would cost me a lot more than here.'

The Reverend T. J. Williams was the minister of two Baptist chapels in the Valley. Every Sunday he would walk four miles across the Valley from one to the other.

'This is a very good area religiously – very, very faithful. There may be yachting and fishing if the reservoir is built, but from a religious point of view, we don't gain anything. It will upset the community. This is a religious area, chapel going, and there will be people coming to work on the dam who will be just the reverse.'

Both he, and the Reverend Hefin Williams, his Presbyterian counterpart in the Valley, said that their chapels were among the best attended in Wales. If the reservoir came, they believed they would lose scores of members, who would be forced to move away. This could not, and should not, be countenanced in a community inextricably linked to the soil.

Chapter Five

Preparation for the Inquiry

During the latter part of 1969, it was announced that there was to be a Public Inquiry. A provisional date was set for 18 November 1969 but was later changed to accommodate the Welsh Office. The Inspector was to be a Mr G. M. Jones.

The thought of a Public Inquiry was terrifying since we had no idea where to begin. It became obvious that we needed professional help if we were to succeed. My father had experience of a Public Inquiry into the proposed flooding of the Senni Valley in Breconshire and had seen at first hand how complicated it could be.

We eventually decided to seek the services of Gareth Morgan, a partner in Milwyn Jenkins and Jenkins, Solicitors of Llanidloes. He already had many of the Dulas Valley residents as his clients. One newspaper described him as 'the young solicitor who is fighting for the Valley dwellers.' On 10 November he came to a meeting of the Dulas Valley Defence Committee and immediately thereafter set about intensive preparations. In an initial telephone conversation with Emlyn Hooson QC, Liberal MP for Montgomeryshire, he concluded that it would be impossible to prepare our case in five weeks and that an adjournment was necessary. He sought the support of

Tudor Watkins, then Labour MP for Brecon and Radnor, and David Gibson Watt, the Conservative MP for Hereford, who lived locally. An application was made with cross-party support in Parliament and the Secretary of State for Wales, George Thomas, granted their request. A new date was fixed for 24 February following. Mr Thomas, however, refused to meet the residents' legal costs. This was a dilemma. We were neither wealthy nor influential people and we had no resources to pay professional witnesses to bring in their expertise. Time was of the essence – but how were we going to pay for such help?

We decided to set up a fighting fund. Two members of the Defence Committee, the Reverend John Pugh and Emrys Evans, agreed to do a house to house collection in the Valley. One hundred and forty-seven families donated sums ranging from five shillings to fifty pounds. We were delighted when the fund reached the princely sum of one thousand, one hundred and thirty-two pounds and one shilling. The community had come up trumps.

It was still insufficient, nevertheless, to cover our costs and on 20 December, Gordon Pugh and my father launched an appeal in the press on behalf of the Dulas Valley Public Inquiry Defence Fund:

> 'We write to ask for your support for the Dulas Valley Inquiry Defence Fund. The Secretary of State has refused our request to meet the reasonable costs of the Dulas Valley Defence Committee presenting their case at the forthcoming Inquiry. Inevitably therefore, the community involved, whom the Defence Committee represents, are faced with heavy costs if they are to have their case properly prepared and presented. Whatever one's views on the proposals, their merits or demerits, we think that everyone will agree that the people affected should be helped to make sure that their case is

fully explored and presented from their particular viewpoint. We therefore ask you, the public, to rally to the help of the affected community and to send contributions however large or small to the Dulas Valley Inquiry Defence as soon as possible.'

The appeal was supported by both local MPs, Tudor Watkins and Emlyn Hooson.

Dulas Valley fund soars to £1,000

The fighting fund to defend the Dulas Valley in Montgomeryshire and Radnorshire against a reservoir plan has jumped from £200 to more than £1,000 in a month, the chairman of the Valley Defence Committee. Mr. Iorwerth Evans, said last night.

Plaid Cymru have contributed £100.

A public inquiry into a Severn River Authority application to carry out test borings in the valley will open at Llanidloes on Tuesday. There are about 80 objections to the application and it is believed the inquiry could last two or three days.

Donations started arriving from various places as the story spread nationwide. The fund grew by an appreciable amount for the time, some six hundred pounds. We printed conspicuous car stickers – heavy black on a red background. Every vehicle in the area displayed one. They were circulated as far afield as we could cover. Strange though it seemed, our stickers could be seen even in the Midlands, where there were many who were unhappy with

Appeal to nation to save a valley

A national appeal for funds to fight the Severn River Authority's plans to drown the Dulas Valley in Mid-Wales will be launched early next week.

The Dulas Valley defence committee have already received numerous offers of financial help in preparing their case against the construction of a multi-million-gallon regulating reservoir in the Tylwch area on the borders of Montgomeryshire and Radnorshire.

Adjourned

A Welsh Office inquiry into whether the river authority should be allowed to make trial borings in the area was to have opened at Llanidloes on Wednesday but, on the application of the objectors, it has now been put off for three months.

The defence committee's legal adviser, Mr. Gareth Morgan, said last night that a written appeal was being drafted and would be issued early next week.

Mr. Morgan said, "The appeal could well be a success considering the expressions of support and offers of help from inside and outside Wales.

"People are looking at the fight to save the Dulas Valley as being of national importance, and if we succeed it could well change the whole attitude of river authorities, water boards, and the Government towards conservation

SAVE THE DULAS VALLEY

PUBLIC APPEAL ON BEHALF OF THE DULAS VALLEY PUBLIC ENQUIRY DEFENCE FUND

We write to ask for your support for the Dulas Valley Enquiry Defence Fund. The Secretary of State for Wales has refused our request to meet the reasonable costs of the Dulas Valley Defence Committee presenting their case at the forthcoming Enquiry.

Inevitably, therefore, the community involved, whom the Defence Committee represents, are faced with heavy costs if they are to have their case properly prepared and presented. Whatever one's views on the proposals, their merits or demerits, we think that everyone will agree that the people affected should be helped to make sure that their case is fully explored and presented from their particular viewpoint.

We therefore ask you, the public, to rally to the help of the affected community and to send contributions however large or small, to the Dulas Valley Enquiry Defence Fund as soon as possible.

T. I. EVANS,
Chairman.

G. P. PUGH,
Secretary.

J. P. PRICE,
Treasurer.

TUDOR WATKINS,
Member of Parliament for Brecon and Radnor.

EMLYN HOOSON,
Member of Parliament for Montgomeryshire.

Contributions should be sent to the Treasurer Mr. J. P. Price, c/o Barclays Bank Limited, 1 Great Oak Street, Llanidloes, Montgomeryshire quoting Account Number 30899569.

the River Authority's proposals. Such empathy hugely boosted our morale. Letters of support came on a daily basis from as far afield as Middlesex, Kent and Essex. It was this response from the public which made us realise that we had something worth fighting for – we should not give up hope.

The more pessimistic felt that the 'high authorities' always succeeded in getting what they wanted, but we were bolstered by many letters of encouragement. One wrote, 'I saw your programme on TV tonight and I beg you to fight and fight to preserve your own beautiful, peaceful way of life.' Another said, 'I would like you to know how much I sympathise with you. Listening and watching on TV made me very sad.' Yet another – 'My wife and I saw the programme on television on Tuesday night about the flooding of your valley and we feel upset about the situation.' One particular enthusiast wrote, 'As 24 February draws nearer, I can sense the atmosphere in the Dulas

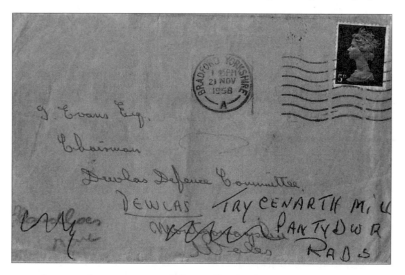

Letters of support arrived from all over the country – this one from Yorkshire eventually found its way!

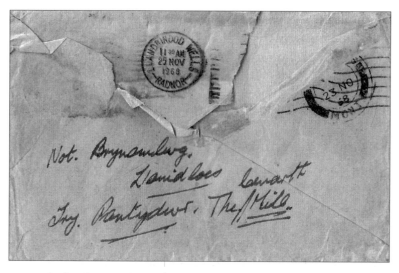

The local Post Office did their best to ensure that such letters reached their destination

Valley and I hope it is electric with a fervent desire to impress upon the Inspector who is to conduct the Inquiry that there is more to the question he is called upon to decide than just whether the Severn River Authority should be allowed to drill holes and discover whether the Valley is suitable to house a reservoir.'

At that time, in the run-up to the Inquiry, my father was celebrating his birthday while in hospital. A gentleman in the next bed wished him a happy birthday and was moved to verse: '. . . *and many more, I wish my friend, till one hundred is the tally – and may your arm be strong to fight to save the Dulas Valley!*' Poetry is ingrained into the Welsh psyche – and can, it would seem, even manifest itself in hospital wards!

Two people came forward to help us with their expertise. Professor Harold Carter, a lecturer at Aberystwyth University, agreed to carry out a demographic survey of the Valley, along the lines pioneered by his predecessor Alwyn Rees in 1950 for the north Montgomery village of Llanfihangel yng Ngwynfa. Together with his colleague Roy Lewis, he set about producing a report which covered all aspects of the Valley from a sociological viewpoint. At the same time, Gareth Morgan was working extremely hard on the case. It was felt that to strengthen our chances, we needed a civil engineer who could challenge the River Authority's proposals and put forward alternative suggestions. Accordingly, he commissioned Dr E. M. Wilson, Reader in Civil Engineering at Salford University, to advise us on the technical details. He committed a great deal of his spare time to produce an alternative scheme.

The proposed flooding of another Welsh valley had become an extremely hot potato on the political stage and stirred up great emotion throughout Wales. We did not think this was necessarily helpful to our cause. Gordon Pugh and my father, Iorwerth Evans, asked on behalf of the Committee for political demonstrators to stay away from the Inquiry. They issued a strong statement:

'The Committee wish it to be known that they are totally opposed to any demonstration taking place during the Public Inquiry. They feel that they have a very strong case on its merits and are particularly anxious that this should not be prejudiced by any irresponsible, unnecessary or disorderly actions on the part of people who may be politically motivated.'

Everything was moving at a frantic pace. Gareth Morgan was besieged by press reporters. He was focused on preparing members of the Defence Committee who had been chosen to give evidence with proofs of their statements. He was engaged with the professional advisers. His preparation took him to the National Library at Aberystwyth and to the offices of the Montgomeryshire Young Farmers' Club. The local MPs were interviewed and an excellent and detailed Brief to Counsel prepared. I was Mr Morgan's secretary at the time and I saw how his files on the case were growing larger by the hour. All this took place in just over three months.

But everybody was fully committed. We knew this was our only chance and that the outcome of the Inquiry could set an important precedent for other cases of this nature. As the support from everywhere grew, so our determination increased. The flooding of the Valley had been a deep concern for several years but during these final weeks of preparation, we thought of nothing else but confronting and countering the threat looming over us.

I think the press got the message. The *Western Mail* reported:

'As one drives through this pleasant, fertile valley which

lies between Rhayader and Llanidloes, one sees a church here, a pub there, a farmhouse half hidden in the folds of a hill, a village school standing in isolation, all creating an impression of emptiness. But out of this apparent vacuum has risen a group of astute and well organised defenders, determined to show at the Public Inquiry that behind the seemingly haphazard spread of farms and cottages, there exists a lively community which contributes to the wealth and culture of the whole region.'

Many were the prayers said individually and in our local chapels throughout this difficult period of our lives. The uncertainty had been hanging over us for years and the heartache and mental strain were enormous. There was a long road ahead, but at least, we felt, we had it well mapped out.

Chapter Six

The Concert

Everyone concerned in the defence of the Dulas thought it a good idea to hold a concert on the eve of the Inquiry and raise more money with entry charges to boost the fighting fund. We planned it to take place in the Community Centre in Llanidloes where the Inquiry was to start on the following morning. Tickets were printed, charging three shillings for adults and one shilling and sixpence for the under fifteens. They sold out like hot cakes.

Music prelude to dam battle

Western Mail Reporter

Young people from the Dulas Valley are to stage a musical first round in the battle to save their homes from the threat of being flooded by a multi-million gallon reservoir.

On Tuesday, February 24, barristers and officials from both sides will thrash out their differences at a public inquiry at the Community Centre, Llanidloes, into the application of the Severn River Authority to make trial borings in the area.

Cultural talent

But on the eve of the inquiry, young residents of Tylwch district on the Montgomeryshire — Radnorshire border, the area affected by the proposed dam, will stage a concert at the community centre. Officials of the Severn River Authority will probably be asked to attend as special guests.

Mr Gareth Morgan, legal adviser to the Dulas Valley Defence Committee, said yesterday: "The variety concert will show what the cultural talent of the locality involves."

Members of Llidiard-y-Waun Young Farmers' Club, who come from the Tylwch area,

are helping to stage the concert. The club has won the county shield in the Montgomeryshire federation annual eisteddfod five times in succession.

Mr. Morgan said the cultural qualities of the area had often been referred to by defenders of the valley. "We will now show their talent as well as talk about it."

Proceeds from the concert will go towards the valley's defence fund. Mr. Morgan said that the fund now had more than £1,500.

The excellent [...] committee [...] sented by [...] inquiry. Mr. [...] of Chester. [...] engaged to [...] the defence [...]

COMPLIMENTARY

Community Centre, Llanidloes

VARIETY CONCERT

given by Residents of the Dulas Valley
supported by Llidiart-y-waen Y.F.C. Choir

Monday, 23rd February, 1970

Doors open at 7 p.m. to commence at 7.30

President : Dr. J. A. Davies, Bangor

ADMISSION 3/- (15 and under 1/6)
Proceeds towards Valley Defence Funds

Finding performers was easy. There were several families and individuals in the community who were practised entertainers. Some had already made recordings and appeared on television. Everyone wanted to do their bit for the cause. Rehearsals began in earnest with our local Rhydd Hywel Youth Choir of Young Farmers leading the way. The choir was named after a hill which overlooked part of the proposed reservoir site. 'Rhydd' means 'free' – would we be set free from the threat hanging over us?

The activity was hectic. I am not sure how our household survived the onslaught, especially with Christmas intervening. My father, as Chair of the Defence Committee, was under great pressure. My mother was conducting the choir and trying to lick it into shape. I was spending much of my life at the office, involved up to my neck in preparations but enjoying every minute of it. The fight was on.

The programme for the concert took shape. The choir were rehearsing Robert Herrick's lyrics 'Daffodils' set to music by Mansel Thomas; Ambrose Lloyd's 'Teyrnasoedd y ddaear', Ceiriog's 'Pe Cawn i Hon' and other pieces – including, with some asperity, 'Oh Dear, What can the Matter Be'. I myself, together with the daughter of the Secretary to the Defence Committee, Helen Pugh, and Lorna Evans of Nanteos, volunteered some rousing recitations. My brother Gareth, Alan Jones of Ystradolwyn and Ann Williams of Lower Fedw were billed as soloists and there were duets on the piano from the Francis sisters of Glan-yr-afon, Dorothy and Gwyneth. I was also to sing as one of a trio with my sister Avril and Ann Williams and lyrics were specially written for a family offering. Cnych Mawr family also provided the trio of Aubrey, Denise and Maralyn Powell. The three chapels under threat of flooding – Sychnant, Nantgwyn and Beulah – were each charged with contributing items. With a ladies' choir and a male quartet as well, it was a comprehensive effort by the community, reflecting our deeply held concern and commitment.

On the night, we gathered together behind the stage. Everyone was extremely nervous, yet excited. Beyond the curtains, we could hear the chatter from an audience waiting expectantly to applaud our efforts, and to unite

COUNTY TIMES & EXPRESS & GAZETTE, Saturday, February 28th, 1970

Dulas Valley bursts into song on eve of inquiry

A thousand people crammed in Llanidloes Community Centre for the concert on Monday given by families from the threatened Dulas Valley.

The defence committee which had organised the concert on the eve of the Public Inquiry which could well decide the fate of the valley had invited its opponents but none of them turned up.

They had wanted to see the talent that will be uprooted if the river authority gets permission to flood the valley.

Members of Llidiartywaen Y.F.C. whose members come from the valley were also taking part and most of the Evans family of Cenarth Mill were on the stage. Mrs Evans, wife of the defence committee chairman, conducted the choir.

Mr Iorwerth Evans, the chairman, said: "It was a highly successful concert."

As well as showing the talent of the valley the concert also made more than £100 for the defence fund.

It was revealed at the concert that Mr Emlyn Hooson Q.C. M.P. had offered his services to the committee. Mr Gordon Pugh the secretary, said: "He will give his professional services as his contribution to the defence fund.

"He decided to do this in the light of the Secretary of State's failure to meet the legal costs of the committee's representation at the inquiry."

When the inquiry opened the next morning Mr B.L. Brough, the Ministry Inspector hearing it thanked the committee for their invitation to the concert. It showed the spirit in which the inquiry was to be conducted and he said he knew they would appreciate why he could not attend.

Part of the choir which took part in the Dulas Valley Concert in Llanidloes Community Centre on Monday. The conductor is Mrs. Iorwerth Evans (right) wife of the defence committee chairman.

Mr. Michael Davies M.C. checks over the programme with men who took part in the concert.

Mr. Alun Jones, Llangurig and Mrs. Jean Woosnam of Pantydwr, both well known Eisteddfodau winners who sang at the Dulas Valley Concert.

Marion Evans, Avril Evans and Mrs. Ann Williams who sang 'Three Little Maids From School' at the concert.

Dulas opponents miss the concert

Officials of the Severn River Authority who had been invited to a concert given by the people from the threatened Dulas Valley on the eve of the public inquiry into the authority's application to carry reservoir site tests in the valley failed to turn up last night.

But the Ministry inspector, who will hear the inquiry, Mr B. Brough, who was also invited, sent a letter apologising for his absence due to pressure of work.

More than 1,000 people crammed into the Community Centre at Llanidloes where the inquiry opens this morning.

Mr Iorwerth Evans, chairman of the Defence Committee, said they had invited the authority officials so that they could see what talent would be lost if the valley was flooded.

Mr Emlyn Hooson, QC, Liberal MP for Montgomery, will appear with Mr Martin Thomas for the Defence Committee.

Mr Gordon Pugh, the secretary, said: "Mr Hooson will be giving his professional services as his contribution to the defence fund."

with us in the hope and fervour we were giving to our performances. We were determined to do our best when the curtains opened. The fighting fund desperately needed the cash.

You can imagine how disappointed we were when word came through that the Inquiry Inspector and the representatives of the River Authority had sent their apologies. After all, we intended the concert to showcase to them the talent within the Dulas Valley. But at least our own legal representatives were there and we were very pleased about that.

Up went the curtains on the main choir: the sea of faces confronting us was undoubtedly a shock. The hall was full to capacity. But as the concert flowed on, we relaxed and began to enjoy ourselves. Speeches were interposed between the songs and entertainment. Our President, Dr J. A. Davies of Bangor, Director of Education for Montgomeryshire, moved us with his passion for Wales and for our little valley. Then it was announced that Emlyn Hooson would not charge for his professional services. He declared that it was his personal contribution to the defence fund in the light of the refusal by the Secretary of State to meet our legal costs. We were overwhelmed by his generosity. We knew we could not have anyone better leading the case. His ability was legendary and his personal, in-depth knowledge of the community would be invaluable. We had been anxious that we would have to raise upwards of three thousand pounds for his standard fees, a large sum in those days. He was to be accompanied by another, extremely able young man as his Junior Counsel, Martin Thomas – nowadays better known as Lord Thomas of Gresford. He had only been in practice at the Bar for two years and this must undoubtedly have been a big test for him personally. But he clearly savoured the challenge and executed it with the utmost feeling and professionalism.

The concert was a resounding success that had all but brought the roof down. Someone later joked that it said much about those who had built the Community Hall! We were all quietly pleased with the way everything had gone – my mother for one was reduced to tears by the manner of the choir's singing. It was a highly charged and emotional evening.

Newspapers reported that the concert had exceeded expectations, with a thousand people present. That may be a little exaggerated but I am sure it was the largest audience ever to have gathered at the Llanidloes Community Centre. The way in which the National Anthem was sung at the close was said in one paper to have excelled in fervour anything the National Eisteddfod could produce. Perhaps the success of the evening, we hoped, would prove a harbinger of better things to come.

We had done our best for the Valley and now it was for our trusted professionals and for those of us due to give evidence to get us through this ordeal.

Chapter Seven

The Public Inquiry

The Inquiry commenced at 10.30 am on Tuesday 24 February 1970. We were naturally apprehensive, but our spirits were high. We had the support of expert professionals who really cared for our case. While Emlyn Hooson and Martin Thomas were covering our interests, there were at least four other barristers representing various bodies, whom we knew to be on our side.

The National Farmers' Union were represented by Counsel, Mr Neville Wallace. He was most anxious to do his best in the case but because he was a Scot domiciled in England, he felt he was out of touch with the Welsh background and ethos. He asked if he could come to the Valley for a weekend before the Inquiry to mingle with the locals and get the 'feel' of the place. I recall he attended a chapel service and various meetings and events and I believe he brought his young family with him.

On the first day of the hearing, just as I was about to leave the office for the Inquiry, I received a call from Gwynfor Edwards, Clerk to the Llanidloes Borough Council. He informed me that the numbers present at the concert the previous night had broken the Fire Regulations. I confess I had a little chuckle: such a minor transgression meant nothing compared with the importance of the day ahead. Off I went to the Inquiry, armed with my shorthand notebooks, my pencils and my determination. My job was to be on hand should anything be needed from the office, just a quick sprint away. During the Inquiry, I was to spend much of my time sprinting.

Mr. B. I. Brough, the Ministry Inspector who is conducting the Inquiry, and who will report his findings to the Secretary of State for Wales.

Lord Thomas of Gresford

Outside the Community Centre, members of Plaid Cymru were congregated for a photograph. I declined their invitation to join them, knowing that the Defence Committee did not want to make our case a political football. The hall was not entirely full: some of the Dulas people were completing their usual morning farming chores as life had to go on. But within a short time, numbers grew considerably and everyone became engrossed, listening intently to the proceedings. Throughout the nine days that the Inquiry sat, daily attendance often reached two hundred and fifty people and was never less than fifty. Most were local, but many came who had taken an interest in our story and simply wanted to observe how the case was going.

The original Welsh Office Inspector, G. M. Jones, was ill and unable to attend. His place was taken by Mr Brian Brough, a member of the Institute of Water Engineers. He seemed to us to be a pleasant enough man but we could not help having some reservations about him as he sat behind his desk on the stage, peering down upon us. It was he who would decide our future. He opened the Inquiry by thanking the Defence Committee for their invitation to the concert. He thought we would appreciate why he was unable to accept. Moving to the issues in the case, he said that although the River Authority's application was simply for permission to make test borings, he was willing to listen to a much wider range of evidence and to report his conclusions to the Secretary of State.

The Authority's case was based on establishing three points:

   (a)   The demand for water after 1978 could not be met from existing sources;

   (b)   The increased demand must be met by water from the Severn;

   (c)   Economic and technical factors made a *prima facie* case for a regulating reservoir.

We objected on all three points, but particularly the last.

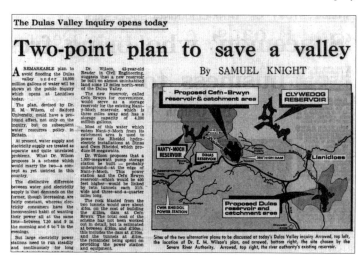

The Dulas Valley inquiry opens today

Two-point plan to save a valley

By SAMUEL KNIGHT

A REMARKABLE plan to avoid flooding the Dulas valley under 18,000 million gallons of water will be shown at the public inquiry which opens at Llanidloes today.

The plan, devised by Dr. E. M. Wilson, of Salford University, could have a profound effect, not only on the inquiry, but on subsequent water resources policy in Britain.

At present, water supply and electricity supply are treated as separate and quite unrelated problems. What Dr. Wilson proposes is a scheme which would marry the two—a concept as yet untried in this country.

The distinctive difference between water and electricity supply is that demands on the former, though increasing, are fairly constant, whereas electricity consumers have the inconvenient habit of wanting their power all at the same time—between 7.30 and 9 in the morning and 6 to 7 in the evenings.

But large electricity power stations need to run steadily and continuously for long

Dr. Wilson, 42-year-old Reader in Civil Engineering, suggests that a new reservoir be built on almost uninhabited land some 12 miles north-west of the Dulas Valley.

The new reservoir, called Cefn Brwyn for convenience, would serve as a storage reservoir for the existing Nant-y-Moch reservoir, which is three miles away and has a storage capacity of 4,200 million gallons.

Most of this water which enters Nant-y-Moch from its catchment area is used to power the Rheidol hydro-electric installations at Dinas and Cwm Rheidol, which produce 56 megawatts.

Dr. Wilson proposes that a 1,000-megawatt pump storage station be built — probably underground—at the edge of Nant-y-Moch. This power station and the Cefn Brwyn reservoir—which would be 400 feet higher—would be linked by twin tunnels each 31ft. wide and three-and-a-quarter miles long.

The rock blasted from the two tunnels would save about £8m. on the cost of building the £16m. dam and Cefn Brwyn. The total cost of the scheme has not been worked out in detail but is estimated at between £33m. and £50m. This includes the dam at £16m., and the tunnels at £5m., the remainder being spent on providing the power station and equipment.

Sites of the two alternative plans to be discussed at today's Dulas Valley inquiry. Arrowed, top left, the location of Dr. E. M. Wilson's plan, and arrowed, bottom right, the site chosen by the Severn River Authority. Arrowed, top right, the river authority's existing reservoir.

In opening his application, Mr Michael Mann QC for the River Authority said that it had been thought originally that the Clywedog Reservoir, some ten miles away would meet the needs of Midland towns until 1981. Now it appeared that another reservoir would be needed by 1978, since the demand for water would increase in certain areas, due to increases in population and changes in standards of living. The Radcliffe Maude Reports had forecast that the demand for water would double by the end of the century. The Authority were aware that a reservoir built in the Valley would cause hardship to the residents and that disruption was regretted. However, the only other alternative, the Gam Valley in north Montgomeryshire, would be far too costly to develop. It would cost two million pounds more.

We were confirmed in our belief that money was the paramount consideration, without any thought of the consequences for the people affected. His were hollow words, which simply gave rise to deep mistrust amongst us.

He explained that tests in the Dulas would take between four and six months. The River Authority would need to carry out drilling and trenching in the Valley. A twelve foot high, three hundred foot long embankment would be built of local rock. Everything would eventually be reinstated – except that a few marking poles would be left in place. It would be for somebody else – the Secretary of State or Parliament itself – to decide whether the Midlands were to have their water supplies put at risk; somebody else, not the River Authority, would have to decide how any deficiencies in water supply were to be met. As far as he knew, no one had put forward any alternative suggestions other than by regulating the River Severn. If the Severn were to be chosen, it was essential to know whether a reservoir in the Dulas Valley was feasible. It was, he said, 'a matter of urgency.'

Witnesses from the Water Authorities of Bristol, Birmingham and Wolverhampton were called in support. In cross-examination by Martin Thomas, they agreed that the site of the River Authority's next reservoir was immaterial to them, as long as they could be guaranteed an adequate supply of water for the future. South Staffordshire and Birmingham stated that they supplied water to one twentieth of the country's population. 'We will need more water by 1978. It must come from the Severn, but where on the Severn does not concern us.' Birmingham Water would need additional supplies at the beginning of 1980, but there were no proposals for the Wye River Authority to supply Birmingham. The witness agreed that it was technically feasible to draw water from the Wye and there was a vast possibility for expansion of the resources it already enjoyed above Rhayader. The Bristol Waterworks Company claimed that the Severn

River Authority would have to honour their commitment to supply them with thirty million gallons a day.

It was the case for the applicant Authority that the Dulas was a high rainfall area. But my father, who happened to be the local Meteorological Office climate recorder, contradicted this spurious contention with the facts. He had himself been recording the figures for many years and was well qualified to refute such an assertion.

Mr Inge, also appearing as a witness for the River Authority, argued that the community was divided. His impression was that the very nature of the valley spurs and the division of the Valley between the counties of Radnor and Montgomery led to his conclusion. When cross-examined by Tasker Watkins, VC, QC on behalf of the Radnor County Council and the Rural Councils of Rhayader, Newtown and Llanidloes, Mr Inge admitted that he had spent no more than two days in the Dulas Valley making his inspection. When asked if two days' acquaintance gave him the right to say that it was a 'divided community', he replied it was the impression he had been given – but then he admitted his opinion was largely based on the geographical nature of the Valley. 'When I tell you,' said Mr Watkins, 'that this is a close-knit community, you would not be in a position to deny it?' 'No,' replied Mr Inge. Mr Watkins made it clear that the local authorities he represented were objecting not out of a desire to prevent water from Wales going to England, but because they were proud of the Dulas Valley. The destruction of such a community, by continuing with the project, would be an act of vandalism.

The next witness, Norman Rowntree, spoke for the Water Resources Board. He told the Inquiry that if there were to be any certainty of meeting the demands on the Severn's resources in and after 1978, the proposed site would have to be investigated immediately. The result would have to be ready for the Board's Report on Wales and the Midlands by 1971 so that the decision could be taken whether or not to construct a reservoir in the Dulas. 'It is essential,' he said, 'that at least one site should be available for early construction to meet demands in the late 1970s.'

The evidence of Mr Phillips of Binnie and Partners, the Westminster Consultant Engineers who had prepared reports for the River Authority, was that although the development in the Dulas would cause considerable disruption, only the Gam Valley site was significantly better from an agricultural and sociological point of view – but the cost would be much greater. This emphasis on cost echoed the earlier submissions of Michael Mann QC in his opening remarks.

Mr Haines, the River Authority's Chief Engineer, was questioned by Emlyn Hooson. He agreed that the Clywedog Reservoir facilities had not, despite costing five million pounds, been fully called upon so far. 'But,' he said, 'if the last summer's dry spell had lasted for the year, then they would have been brought into action.' Mr Hooson explained to the Inspector that when the Clywedog site was investigated, the year 1968 was described as the crucial year, just as 1978 was described as crucial for the Dulas scheme. He put it to Mr Haines that no new reservoir was needed, but Mr Haines disagreed. Mr Hooson suggested that the water authorities were notorious for over-insuring. 'If you want an additional "insurance policy", you could flood an uninhabited area in the Upper Severn belonging to the Forestry Commission which would provide four million gallons. This water and the untapped resources of Clywedog would keep supplies going up to 1988.' Mr Haines admitted that apart from an exceptionally dry year, the water in the Clywedog might not be needed until 1980. It was an admission raising loud applause from the apprehensive audience in the Community Centre. However, Mr Haines would not accept Mr Hooson's suggestion that incorrect estimates for the Clywedog meant that the Dulas figures were also incorrect.

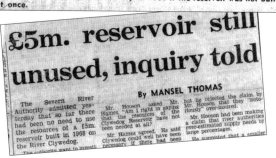

USE OF FORESTRY COMMISSION SOURCE WOULD GIVE WATER UNTIL 1988

Dam not needed for some years, Inquiry told

THE WATER from the Clywedog Reservoir would n o t be needed before 1980, despite a claim in 1965 that supplies to West Midlands and other Severn towns would run dry in 1968 if the reservoir was not built at once.

£5m. reservoir still unused, inquiry told

By MANSEL THOMAS

The Severn River Authority admitted yesterday that so far there had been no need to use the resources of a £5m. reservoir built in 1968 on the River Clywedog. The authority want to invest...

Mr. Hooson asked Mr. Haines "Am I right in saying that the resources of the Clywedog Reservoir have not been needed at all?

Mr. Haines agreed. He said Clywedog could well have been necessary if there had been

but he rejected the claim by Mr. Hooson that they "notoriously" over-insured.

Mr. Hooson had been making a claim that river authorities over-estimated supply needs by large percentages.

He suggested that a smaller

CALL FOR WATER CONTROL

A call for autonomy for Wales on the question of water resources has been made to the Secretary of State for Wales by Montgomeryshire landowners.

"Wales should be allowed to govern itself in the matter of water resources and the Welsh committee of the Water Resources Board should be autonomous," the letter says.

They also demand the same compensation for property flooded by reservoirs as for property sold for private development.

Report attacked

In a letter to Mr. George Thomas the Montgomeryshire branch of the Country Landowners' Association say that the person dispossessed of land has to re-establish himself in the private market.

"More of the receipts from the sales of water should be pumped back into the area of conservation by way of amenities," the letter says.

It also attacks the Welsh Council pilot report on land use strategy in Mid-Wales.

● The inquiry into the Severn River Authority's application to investigate the Dulas Valley as a potential reservoir site resumes at Llanidloes today.

Mr Haines told the Inquiry that the Authority was preparing a survey into possible ways of conserving and developing water resources. But he envisaged that it was unlikely to reveal any method of meeting demands, other than by further regulation of the Severn. Estuarine barrages and desalination processes did not appear to provide a short-term answer to the problem. He realised that a reservoir would affect people's lives and that there would be a loss of land to agriculture and food production, but he claimed that a reservoir could bring considerable benefits in terms of flood relief, amenities, recreational use and the tourist industry. He added that since Clywedog had been put into operation, there had been a marked decrease in flooding in the upper reaches of the Severn and an additional reservoir would decrease it further.

Emlyn Hooson raised another obstacle to the proposals. The Mid Wales gas grid ran for some two and a half miles through the proposed site. He also pointed out that although the River Authority were prepared to spend ninety-five thousand pounds on trial borings, they had spent no money in carrying out a sociological survey of the community they were bent on destroying. That demonstrated to us yet again where the Authority's priorities lay.

A row broke out about the final reports which had been commissioned by the River Authority from the Consultant Engineers, Binnie and Partners, on ten possible reservoir sites in Mid Wales. Counsel for the Montgomery County Council, Patrick Freeman, asked for the disclosure of these reports. Michael Mann vigorously objected. 'I regard the withholding of information from the public and Minister,' said Mr Freeman, 'to be a denial of my rights in justice to pursue my case on behalf of the County Council.' Mr Mann replied that disclosure of the reports was against the public interest. The Inspector, Mr Brough, initially refused the disclosure application. Mr Freeman protested, saying that his clients would consider overnight whether to withdraw from the Inquiry altogether. In response, the Inspector emphasised that he did not rule out the possibility that the Inquiry might have to meet in private session to look at the reports.

After much discussion, Mr Brough eventually ordered that the reports should be produced. After argument, he now considered that it was indeed in the public interest that this be done. The reports were produced and distributed to objectors at the end of day two, so that they could read them overnight. It emerged that the Dulas and the Gam Valleys, some thirty miles apart, were both suitable for the construction of the next Severn regulating reservoir. On the question of land quality and the number of farms, property and people displaced, the Gam was more favourable, as Mr Phillips of Binnie's had admitted in his earlier evidence. But the cost of developing that site would be between £2,500,000 and £3,400,000 – forty to sixty-five per cent more than the proposed Dulas scheme. We now understood why the files of the Severn River Authority were housed overnight in Llanidloes Police Station throughout the Inquiry 'for safe keeping'.

That was the extent of the case for the applicants, the River Authority. It was now our turn to place our evidence and argument before the Inquiry.

18 WELSH NEWS, CLASSIFIED ADVERTISE!

THE DULAS VALLEY

INQUIRY: DAY 3

Secret file on 10 dam sites freed

By MANSEL JONES

A consultants' report on 10 possible reservoir sites in Mid-Wales valleys, which has been kept secret for almost two years, was made public last night.

The move was ordered yesterday by Mr. B. I. Brough, the Welsh Office inspector, at the Dulas Valley inquiry at Llanidloes. Copies of the report, on which the Severn River Authority based their decision to test the valley for their next regulating reservoir, were distributed to objectors at the end of yesterday's session.

POLICE KEEP NIGHT GUARD ON FILES

Police are keeping an overnight guard on the files of the Severn River Authority during the Dulas Valley inquiry at Llanidloes.

After the hearing ends each day, officials of the river authority take their documents to the local police station 100 yards away. There they are kept in the cells until the inquiry resumes the following morning.

The river authority's chief engineer, Mr. Leslie Haines, said they had "a special arrangement." Details of the arrangement would not be of public interest, he added.

A police spokesman at Llanidloes said yesterday the authority had asked if they could keep their files in the police station. This was a facility the police would offer to anyone wanting to keep property in safe keeping, the spokesman said.

Gas grid in dam site, says Hooson

By MANSEL JONES

The Mid-Wales gas grid runs through the area of the Dulas Valley where the Severn River Authority want to build a reservoir to supply water for the West Midlands, it was revealed yesterday.

A warning that this could affect the cost of the reservoir scheme was given by the M.P. for Montgomeryshire, Mr. Emlyn Hooson.

He is the barrister representing the valley's defence committee at the Llanidloes public inquiry into the river authority's application to make tests in the valley.

The four-inch steel grid main was laid in 1960 to carry gas to Rhayader, Llandrindod Wells and Builth Wells.

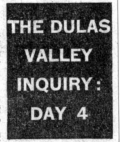

THE DULAS VALLEY INQUIRY: DAY 4

"They sat down and resolved that it was undesirable and might even amount to an act

First up was Gordon Pugh. He had started farming with five hundred acres but had built up his holdings to eight hundred. 'As residents and farmers,' he said, 'we view the proposals of the Severn River Authority with alarm. Indeed, I am forced to say that we are living under a cloud of suspense and blight. I ask you to consider the heartache and mental strain that has already been caused. If a reservoir were to be constructed, the future not only of this valley, but of the whole area would be in jeopardy. It would lose a large portion of its indigenous population – people this part of Mid Wales cannot afford to lose at any cost. We do not believe the River Authority want this desecration upon their conscience. If they do, then men will judge them not as builders, but as despoilers of the heartland of Wales. We believe our case is just and right. We appeal to the Secretary of State never to let the monstrosity of a dam rear its ugly head in our valley.'

J. W. Price pointed out that two hundred and fifteen

people would be affected by a reservoir and its aqueducts. Not all would lose their homes. There were sixty-eight people living in properties that would be drowned. Fifteen farms would be submerged; other property would be so near the high water mark of the reservoir that those residents would have to move.

The Baptist Minister, the Reverend T. J. Williams, told the Inspector that sailing, fishing and the gains from tourism were a poor exchange for the Valley in its present guise. Its people were industrious, talented and loyal to their chapels. Four Chapels would be affected – two were Baptist – Nantgwyn with a membership of one hundred and twenty-one, and Beulah with eighty-nine. There were fifty-eight members of the Presbyterian church at Sychnant and Hendreaur had a Sunday School of about twelve members. Young people's appreciation for life's higher values and interests was a heartening feature of the district. To lose any of the inhabitants would aggravate the drift from rural areas where the farmers had worked hard to improve their farms.

He was followed by my father, Iorwerth Evans. He too spoke of the neighbourliness of the Valley and its religious, social and cultural aspects. He referred to the concert on the eve of the Inquiry: 'As well as performances by the Young Farmers' Club, twenty-five individuals performed, either in small groups or individually. The press estimated a thousand people attending, from a forty mile radius.' He asserted that we had tried to maintain a reasonable attitude, but it appeared that we had achieved nothing to alter the River Authority's mind. 'We have the comparison of David and Goliath,' he added and, echoing General Haig's famous Field Order of 1918 to reflect our plight, he concluded, 'With our backs to the wall and believing in the justice of our cause, we will fight to the end.'

Dam could mean mass migration of 300 people

THE PEOPLE of the Dulas Valley would fight to the end to save their land from being turned into a reservoir, Mr. Iorwerth Evans, chairman of the Defence Committee, told the Dulas Inquiry at Llanidloes this week.

The Severn River Authority, which is seeking permission to carry out reservoir site tests, had no idea of the richness of life in the valley, said Mr. Evans.

If the river authority officials and the Inspector, Mr. Brian Brough had attended the eve of inquiry concert given by the people of the valley, they would have seen the community strength and culture which a visit alone to the alley would not reveal. That had been the reason for inviting them.

The religious life of the valley was strong, but a reservoir would destroy this.

The Inquiry heard from Mr. J. W. Price, Pantyswr, that 215 people would be affected by a reservoir and its acqueducts. Not all these would lose their homes. The number of people living in property, that would be under water was 68.

Fifteen farms would be submerged. Other property would be too close to the reservoir and the people would have to move.

Mr. Gordon Pugh, secretary to the Defence Committee, said people

heartening feature of the district.

To lose any of the inhabitants would only aggravate the drift from the rural areas, and the farmers had worked hard and improved their farms.

Ald. Tudor Watkins, Labour M.P. for Brecon and Radnor, also told the Inquiry of the unique community spirit to be found in the Dulas Valley. He added: "I have been acquainted with farming long enough to know a good farming community when I see one, and there is not the slightest doubt that the community of the Dulas Valley deserves that description."

There was a highly developed cultural life, and a great deal of musical talent which performed over a wide area and gave its services readily to charity. "This is a rich rural community and its life should not be disrupted or destroyed lightly," he said.

Ald. Watkins criticised the Secretary of State for not paying for the defence of the valley, and he hoped the position would be remedied in the future.

Mr. Iorwerth Evans "We will fight to the end," he told the Inquiry.

Ald. Watkins agreed with Mr. Michael Mann, for the River Authority, that in 1966 he had advised the people of the valley to allow the survey to take place, but he had now changed his mind. He had been involved in other reservoir projects since and had become wiser.

Daily Post, Thursday, March 5, 1970   7

People of Dulas unite to save their valley

BIRMINGHAM Corporation were not fully utilising their Elan Valley reservoir in Radnorshire, it was claimed at a public inquiry at Llanidloes, yesterday when the defenders of the Dulas valley in Montgomeryshire and Radnorshire closed their ranks against the Severn River authority.

Goliath

Mr Ioweth Evans, chairman of the defence committee, said: "We will not lightly give up this community which will be broken up if these proposals go through.

"We see that Birmingham does not fully utilise the Elan Valley.

"We have tried to maintain a reasonable attitude but it appears that we have achieved nothing against the Severn River Authority, but we have the comparison of David and Goliath, or, if you wish, Naboth and his vineyard to encourage

WELSH AND F...

THE DULAS VALLEY INQUIRY: DAY 7

David v. Goliath fight promised

By MANSEL JONES

The people of the Dulas Valley, once the scene of war-time mock battles, went to the public inquiry at Llanidloes yesterday to fight for their homes and land.

Ministers appealed to a Government inspector not to split their flocks and another drew Biblical comparisons with the Dulas fight.

The leader of the valley fighters also turned to the Bible to make his plea to the inspector.

Emotion

It was a day of emotion at the inquiry into the Severn River Authority's plan to flood the valley for a reservoir.

At the end of the day, when the sometimes impassioned pleas were over, the people of Cwm Dulas had clearly made their point—the reservoir plan would be fought to the bitter end.

Mr. Iorwerth Evans, the Valley Defence Committee's 52-year-old chairman, promised the water seekers a "David and Goliath" fight.

Mr. Evans, who will lose his home if plans to build the reservoir materialise, said, "We will not lightly give up this community.

"The river authority and their supporters have no con-

ception of the riches of life in our valley and the tremendous damage they are doing to the community and to the nation of Wales.

"We have tried to maintain a reasonable attitude in opposition. It appears that we have achieved nothing against the river authority judgment, but we have the comparison of David and Goliath to encourage us.

He felt sure the authorities would be prepared to pay the extra cost of developing one of the many uninhabited sites available.

And he added, "I quote famous words on a critical occasion: 'With our backs to the wall and believing in the justice of our cause, we will fight to the end.'"

Despite the obvious depth of feeling among the valley dwellers who listened with rapt attention to their champions, the composure typical of the Dulas people was maintained. Only a few bursts of applause gave them away.

Alarm

Mr. Gordon Pugh, secretary of the defence committee, who farms 800 acres in the valley and stands to lose most of his best land, told of the cloud of suspense and blight the people had lived under for the past four years.

He said, "We view the pro-

posals of the river authority with alarm.

"I ask you to consider the heartache and mental strain that have already been caused.

"If a reservoir was constructed the future of not only this valley but the whole area would be in jeopardy.

"It would lose a large proportion of its indigenous population—people that this part of Mid-Wales cannot afford to lose at any cost."

Desecration

The disruption created could result in the mass migration of between 200 and 300 people. It would be "a disaster."

Mr. Pugh added, "We do not believe the river authority want this desecration upon their conscience.

"If they do, then men will judge them not as builders but as despoilers of the heartland of Wales.

"We believe our cause is just and right. We appeal to the Secretary of State never to allow the monstrosity of a dam to rear its ugly head in our valley."

The valley's two ministers, the Rev. T. J. Williams, a Baptist, and the Rev. Hefin Williams, a Presbyterian, said their chapels were now among the best attended in Wales. If the reservoir came they could lose scores of members,

On a day when the 66 people attending the Sunday school at Nantgwyn Chapel, Pantydwr became as important as the thirsty millions in the West Midlands, it was not surprising even to hear a Member of Parliament admit he had been wrong.

Mr. Tudor Watkins, M.P. for Brecon and Radnor, gave evidence for Radnorshire County Council of which he is chairman.

He agreed with Mr. Michael Mann, for the river authority that in September 1966 he had told the authority that his advice to his constituents in the Dulas Valley was that they should allow surveys of their land.

Mr. Mann asked, "Is your advice to your constituents still the same?"

Wiser

Mr. Watkins replied, "Certainly not."

He explained, "I have changed my mind. I have become wiser.

"I have come to realise that a survey according to the Water Resources Act is not a visual survey, as I had in mind but one that creates a lot more agricultural disturbance than I thought.

"This is a rich rural community and its life should not be disrupted or destroyed lightly."

A survey of stock numbers within the Valley had been carried out by Michael Davies of Garthfawr. In the years 1968/69, 6,000 sheep had been sold fat and a further 3,700 as stores. During the same period, 120 cattle had gone to market finished, with 640 sold as stores for finishing down country where their quality was much in demand. In March 1969, 14,300 sheep and 1,850 cattle were known to be wintering away. This was a necessary tradition on hill farms where winter fodder might be in short supply due to the weather and the lack of sufficient bottom land to grow it on. He pointed out that the dramatic reduction in bottom land through drowning would render an unacceptable number of farms unviable.

The Member of Parliament for Brecon and Radnor, Tudor Watkins, spoke of the unique community spirit to be found in the Dulas. 'I have been acquainted with farming long enough to know a good farming community when I see one, and there is not the slightest doubt that the community of the Dulas Valley deserves that description. There is a highly developed cultural life and a great deal of musical talent which performs over a wide area and gives its services readily to charity. Not only is it an enchanting and lovely place, but it is populated by a vigorous, lively and gifted community. This is a rich rural community and its life should not be disrupted or destroyed lightly.' He criticised the Secretary of State for not paying for the defence of the Valley and he hoped the position would be remedied in the future. When asked by Mr Mann if in 1966 he had advised the people of the Valley to allow the survey to take place, he replied that he had. However, having been involved in other reservoir projects, he had become wiser and changed his mind.

Mr Wallace for the NFU, submitted with some prescience, 'Perhaps there will come a time when the needs of individuals and individual communities do come to be valued as much as mere money – and when that stage is reached, I suggest that there will be no more Dulas Valleys investigated. If investigations are allowed to go ahead, then we have virtually lost our chance of stopping the reservoir altogether.' The NFU called as a witness Stephen Williams, the liaison officer to the Ministry of Agriculture, who owned a farm on the edge of the proposed reservoir site. He put forward an alternative scheme which would involve forming a network of farm ditches and small dams. This, he claimed, would provide an adequate water supply into the River Severn. He envisaged a series of small lakes surrounded by trees set in the Valley. Channels and ditches would have to be made to store the water that fell on the land. He likened his suggestion to a dry sponge which would absorb water. Likewise, dry soil could store water and be released by these small dams.

The Chairman of the Radnor branch of the Council for the Protection of Rural Wales, John Hunt, spoke of the natural beauty of the countryside as having a value in itself. 'We view with great disquiet the tendency to regard the water of our Welsh valleys as an easy answer to the admittedly high demands for water and we feel that the time has come to call a halt to the drowning of our upland valleys. We feel that there is far too great a readiness to accept the cheap and easy way; to place too great an emphasis on the purely economic factor.'

A most important witness was Professor Harold Carter, who presented the survey which he and Roy Lewis had prepared. It took into account the demographics of the area, the condition of housing and amenities, the pattern of employment and the journey undertaken to shops and services. It looked at the community structure with the patterns of kinship and the nature of the activities in which the people of the community were engaged. Its findings, illustrated by clear graphics and tables, were that although the population of the Dulas Valley was decreasing, the losses were not any more advanced than in any other community in the upland areas of Mid Wales. They could not see any evidence to suggest that farming was in a precarious state. There was an 'obvious dominance' of farming and the services of electrification and household and other amenities were adequately provided for. The survey provided data to demonstrate that there was a very strong community consciousness and a tight network of family relationships. Apart from the fact that English and not Welsh was the dominant language, the area was in all respects a Welsh community with a life and feeling of its own.

We certainly knew that there were strong Welsh traditions throughout the community. Historically, the westernmost part of Radnorshire in particular had been the last within the county where Welsh was routinely spoken. A gradual westerly erosion had taken place throughout the county over a long period due to proximity with the English border. This was later exacerbated as a result of the construction in Victorian times of the Elan Valley Dams nearby, when significant numbers of English speaking stonemasons and labourers had been imported from elsewhere. Only one witness at the Inquiry took the opportunity to give his evidence in Welsh. That was the Reverend D. J. Owen, representing the Upper Montgomery Presbytery.

Professor Carter and Mr Lewis concluded that it was quite inappropriate to think of the area in terms of urban notions and ideas. They made the forceful point that although superficially it might appear to the passer-by to be empty and to have no central point, the richness of the community linkages appeared to be far greater than those in modern suburbia.

Another of our experts, Dr E. M. Wilson of Salford University, presented an alternative scheme which would not only provide water by a regulating reservoir, but would generate cheaper electricity through the pump storage method. The plan involved the joint use by the Severn Water Authority and the Central Electricity Board of a large new reservoir which could be built on almost uninhabited land, some fifteen miles to the north west. This was the land between Nantymoch Reservoir and the Llanidloes area. Nantymoch had a capacity of 4,200 million gallons, most of which was used to power the Rheidol hydro-electric installations at Dinas and Cwm Rheidol. The 56 megawatts of power produced at the time was used in South Wales. Dr Wilson's proposed reservoir to be known as Cefn Brwyn, would have a capacity of up to 48 billion gallons and would be constructed on the headwaters of the Severn and Wye. It could be used as a storage reservoir but would also permit a 1,000-megawatt pump storage power station to be built on the banks of Nantymoch. Two tunnels would be built, one to carry water up to Cefn Brwyn when electricity was cheap at night, the other to carry the flow downwards to power the station when electricity was required during the day. Dr Wilson hoped that although the cost had not been worked out, the scheme could be sympathetically examined before irretrievable decisions were made about the Dulas or any other threatened valley. Predictably, the scheme was dismissed as too expensive. Dr Wilson was in the vein of modern developments of this nature: the Dinorwig scheme in Llanberis built on precisely these principles, began in 1974 and was completed in 1984. It has amply proved its worth.

Not as part of our Defence Committee campaign, but on behalf of Plaid Cymru, Gwynfor Evans, the Plaid leader, made a passionate intervention. He described Government action over water in Wales, flouting Welsh opinion when feelings were running high, as provocative. 'I want to appeal to the Government to replace its high-handed and arrogant attitude with democracy and respect for Welsh opinion. Let it act as a Welsh Government would act.' He criticised the failure to establish a Welsh Water Authority, thereby giving powerful English authorities the right to go ahead with their plans. 'They are now twice blessed,' he said, 'not only do they get the water, but they get it for nothing.' He continued, 'It has been said by Government spokesmen that there could never be another Tryweryn. There obviously will be another Tryweryn – in Cwm

Dulas.' He was followed by Geraint Howells, later to be MP for Ceredigion and a Liberal Democrat peer. He was a very experienced farmer who sympathised with the farming community. He believed that greater benefit would be gained by preserving the Valley for agriculture than by allowing the present proposals to be approved. They would destroy one of the most closely knit and well balanced communities that existed.

David Jones, a past Chairman of the Montgomeryshire Federation of Young Farmers' Clubs provided the Inquiry with the views of young people. Llidiartywaen YFC had been in the forefront of activities within the county, within Wales and at national and international events. He spoke of the success of these young farmers in passing proficiency tests in all sorts of subjects. He pointed out that the Rhydd Hywel Youth Choir, which had originated in that club, had won the Youth Choir Competition at the 1965 National Eisteddfod of Wales, beating such formidable competitors as the London Welsh Youth Choir and Cardiff Aelwyd Choir. He sought to prove that the Dulas Valley was a vibrant cultural community, with principled young people contributing widely to its success and to the greater good.

At the end of the evidence stage of the Inquiry, when all these eloquent and able witnesses had been called, we felt that no single stone had been left unturned. Both Emlyn Hooson and Martin Thomas had been outstanding in defence, as had our own Gareth Morgan. How fortunate we had been to have them. They had handled our case with such verve. Emlyn Hooson was unable to be at the Inquiry for its entire duration due to prior commitments. However, Martin Thomas attended and participated throughout, keeping a close watch on our interests.

In his closing speech, Emlyn Hooson spoke of the value

of the community which would be destroyed. 'It is not obstinacy that makes the people of the Dulas Valley fight as they are fighting. It is the realisation that they are faced with a choice. There is the human price on one side, and the economic price on the other. When you realise that the economic price is a couple of pence a month for the consumer, then there is no doubt in my mind which price should be paid. It is the economic price.' He accused the River Authority of exaggerating the demand for water. If the Secretary of State gave his consent in the face of all this evidence, he would jeopardise all the credibility of his position as the guardian of Wales' interests, and as the umpire to hold the balance between the demands for water – which he fully appreciated to exist – and the deep community interests affected. 'These people would have equal objection to losing their home to a Welsh Water Board who would sell the water, as to any other water board. We would not like to have the strength of our case marred by failure to appreciate the difference between their objection and a political point of view.' He said there appeared to be a complete failure by the Water Board to look into other recommendations and alternatives and continued, 'If the River Authority and the Water Resources Board have no contingency plans to meet demand in 1978, then either they are totally incompetent or the demand just isn't there.'

Martin Thomas in his closing speech was equally passionate. 'There is no reason,' he said, 'why Wales should be sacrificed to provide cheap water.' He contrasted the full and colourful life of the farms, homes, chapels, fields and hedges of the Dulas Valley as it presently existed with the cold, dank and lifeless lake it would become, were it to be drowned. He was surprised, when he looked round at the conclusion of his address, to see many of the audience in tears. But a curious and touching thing then happened. Mr Mann summed up on behalf of the River Authority and marshalled his arguments and his battered evidence as best he could. Then as he sat down, the audience clapped him. Although he represented the enemy, the people present recognised the quality of the man and in their generosity of spirit, so representative of their community, they paid him that compliment.

Meanwhile, newspaper reports made for interesting reading. Some of Geoffrey Newson's analytical comments in the *Daily Express* bordered on the comical:

'With their homes at stake, the farmers at the back of the hall speak among themselves from the heart. And since speaking from the heart is not always the most efficient language of an Official Inquiry, they have put their trust and some of their savings into an intellectual group at the front of the hall who speak from Lincoln's Inn. The champion is Mr Emlyn Hooson QC and MP for Montgomeryshire who is fighting for the Dulas without fee. Valleys like Dulas, with its rigours and romanticism, have produced both the eloquence which makes the Welsh good teachers and the bite which makes them good rugby players. Blend them and you have the reasons why the Welsh also produce good barristers. Mr Hooson has come with the heart additive too. He married 'Noel the Meat's' cousin and lives four miles from the Dulas Valley. The Inquiry Inspector, who should have been a Mr Jones, who is ill, has had to be replaced by a Mr Brian Brough, who is a member of the Institute of Water Engineers. He is an alert, kindly man with darting eyes. He has found himself sharing lodgings in the town's Red Lion Hotel with reporters and, in the delicate jargon of the administrator, he has suggested that he 'will endeavour not to intrude.' The real *intruders* at this Inquiry, the flooders, 'stand out' as they say in Wales, like chapel hat pegs – although it would be truer to say clothes' pegs, as they are all spruced and neatly wrapped in city suits.'

Michael Mann said afterwards that he had never previously known such interest in a matter of this sort. But it was no surprise to us. It was confirmation – if not an admission – from our adversary, of the strength within our community. Whilst we patiently awaited the Secretary of State's decision, the Press continued to take a keen interest and interviews were still being sought. An article in The *Guardian* reported that both my father as Chair of the Defence Committee and the River Authority were equally convinced they would win – whilst, realistically, Gareth Morgan thought that it could go either way.

The *Express* and *Times Gazette*, our local newspaper, wrote:

'The local Defence Committee will fight, but surely they must know the inevitable outcome. The only thing that can save this valley, recently described by the Ministry Inspector as an area of outstanding natural beauty, is a negative result when the site investigations and borings are carried out. Even to a layman, the Dulas Valley is an obvious choice. It is easy to dam and there is no shortage of water. The River Dulas which runs into the Severn is served by at least eight streams.'

My father's comments to one reporter were that the people of the Dulas Valley would fight to the end to save our land from being turned into a reservoir:

'The Severn River Authority, which is seeking permission to carry out reservoir site tests, have no idea of the richness of life in the Valley. If the River Authority officials and the Inspector, Mr Brian Brough, had attended the eve of Inquiry concert given by the people of the Valley, they would have seen the strength and culture of the community which a visit alone to the valley would not reveal. That was the reason for inviting them. I don't begrudge the Midlands people the water they need, but the authorities adopt a colonial attitude and they have not done enough to seek alternatives. I have the unhappy feeling that what we are fighting for, our way of life, does not count with the authorities.'

Throughout the Inquiry, sleepless nights and nail biting became an inevitable feature of our lives. We would simply have to trust that eventually common sense would prevail.

(Martin Thomas' addendum based on his notes from the Inquiry, gives a more detailed account of the proceedings.

Of particular interest are the closing speeches, some of which reflect the emotion felt at the culmination of events).

Chapter Eight

The Wait

They say that a dying man sees his whole life flashing before him. So it was that, as we awaited the outcome of the Inquiry, we reflected upon everything that had happened over past years. A strange analogy perhaps, but we were wholly consumed with apprehension for our valley as we looked back at all the activities and experiences which had taken place within the community.

Music was a notable thread. We had been brought up learning to read tonic sol-fa, now something of the past. It was a strict training which created musicians of note. There were composers, particularly of chapel hymn tunes, and singers and conductors, some of whom had gone on to enjoy professional careers. There were mixed and male voice choirs. Many of us attended weekly music lessons too.

At the weekends, the local hop was pretty strictly disciplined. Occasionally there was the odd tiff between the lads, usually over a girl, but nothing too serious.

Then there was the annual Pantydwr Show, a typical country event which drew in people from the surrounding areas and attracted some 1,000 entries. One of the outdoor activities was the final of the football competition, a knock-out contest spread out over the preceding week.

The sheep and lamb sales every year were another feature – I well remember all the fuss of washing faces and clipping fleeces to make our animals look their best.

The Women's Institute also featured.

The Young Farmers' Club met at Llidiartywaun on a Monday night. Looking back, it was a little segregated – the young men were taught machinery maintenance, stock judging, farm safety and vehicle maintenance, while the girls were organised in groups for cookery, crocheting, floral art, hair-styling, makeup, and hat and doll making. We did come together however for poultry plucking and trussing – and, to be fair, antiques, ballroom dancing, first aid, drama, public speaking and quiz competitions were also a very social part of the proceedings. As I have already mentioned, winning the Youth Choir competition at the National Eisteddfod of Wales in Newtown in 1965 was the absolute tops. The choir also represented the county in the All Wales Festival of Arts and gained first place.

That was not the only success by a long way. We made an extra effort for the Young Farmers' Eisteddfod and in the County Rally. For five consecutive years between 1963 and 1968, we won the County Eisteddfod Shield and were runners up in the following year as well. Gwyneth Pugh won the Bardic Chair twice. In 1967, our team won the County Public Speaking Competition. In 1969, Dorothy Jones (formerly Francis) topped the Arts and Crafts section and followed that by coming third in 'Who Makes the Best Farmer's Wife' competition in the Royal Show at Stoneleigh. Margaret Williams represented Wales in the 4H Rally in Austria in 1969, Gwynfryn Evans was a past Chairman of the County YFC Eisteddfod Committee and Gareth Evans was the county delegate on the Welsh Committee for three years. Avril Evans and I represented Wales at a European Festival held in Germany in 1964, singing in a number of concerts there – subsequently, in 1969, Avril was the County Hostess for Montgomeryshire during the 1969 European Festival of Arts held in Wales. Dressmaking was my particular forte and on four occasions I was proud to have represented Montgomeryshire in the National YFC dressmaking and modelling competition. I was once placed second in the finals held at the Royal Show. This was our own Llidiartywaun club but others from the Valley played an equally active and successful role in a broad range of activities in the Rhayader Young Farmers' Club nearby. Jeff Evans won the All Wales YFC Ploughing Match and then went on to be Ploughman of the Day. He also won the National YFC Sheep Shearing Competition at the Bath and West Show.

In the Urdd Eisteddfod, Avril Evans on three occasions won the Recitation competition for Welsh learners. She and sister Meryl twice won the Duet competition, with brother Gareth once winning the Under 18 Tenor solo. At the 1965 National Eisteddfod in Newtown, the three siblings along with brother Gwynfryn came first in the Quartette competition.

All these pursuits and interests were not forced upon us. They sprang naturally from our rural, self-sufficient upbringing and we thoroughly enjoyed them all.

Outsiders often asked us what we found to do in such a quiet place. The answer was always the same – there were endless things to do and insufficient time to do them! We saw that young urbanites had plenty of amenities with many things organised for them. We country dwellers mastered the art of organising our own entertainment and, just like generations before us, the people of the Dulas Valley struggled to find time to fit it all in. But it was a heritage not just to look back on: our cause was based not on the past, but on the future. It was a labour of love – love of our community and what it stood for, love of our Welsh traditions, love of taking part and, above all, a love of life itself.

We were *never* going to give this up without a fight. What did the Severn River Authority think they were doing?

Glanrafon Halt were my parents would have caught the train to do their shopping in Llanidloes, having first crossed a few fields to get there. How times have changed!

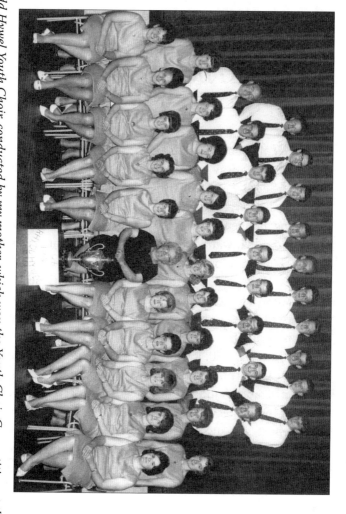

The Rhydd Hywel Youth Choir, conducted by my mother, which won the Youth Choir Competition at the 1965 National Eisteddfod held in Newtown. It was comprised mainly of YFC members including my six siblings and myself.

Chapter Nine

The Decision

The sleepless nights of the long wait stretched on through March all the way to December. We thought that the fate of the Senni Valley in the south of Breconshire, whose Inquiry had preceded ours, would be determined first. But nothing happened. We remembered how the people of Tryweryn had waited for a positive result. But it was all in vain. They had lost their fight, their livelihoods and their homes. How painful that must have been. Nobody told us how we would hear the result – by letter, through our legal representatives, or simply in the newspapers. So we waited . . . and waited.

In June of 1970, a General Election took place and the Labour Government was replaced by a new Conservative administration under Ted Heath. George Thomas, to whom the Inspector, Brian Brough, had already submitted his Report, was succeeded by Peter Thomas as Secretary of State for Wales. This no doubt prolonged the decision. But eventually, on 1 December, Peter Thomas announced that he was rejecting the application to investigate the Dulas site.

The Report stated that although the Inquiry was for site investigations, Mr Brough had found it understandable that the community's case was laid on the basis that they objected to the reservoir itself. His findings were entirely favourable.

'The people of the Dulas Valley form a particularly strong, virile, happy and go-ahead community which would be liable to disintegrate if a reservoir were built there . . . their cases were prepared and presented with a great deal of effort, research and expense without undue emotion . . . a reservoir would put an end to the present way of life and economy of the Valley.'

The Report went on to say that the Upper Severn and Vyrnwy valleys had been blighted:

'. . . all concerned have been bedevilled by uncertainty which cannot be obviated until the outcome of the Wales and Midland study (due to take place next year) is known and until the Authority can decide whether or not to promote a reservoir. The Authority, in the objectors' opinion and in mine, have asked in effect that consideration at the proper time and place of any firm reservoir proposal should not be prejudged now. For in due course Parliament or yourself Sir, (Mr Thomas), may expect to be asked to decide such a proposal without being able to weigh alternatives equally.'

The Inspector discounted objections made at the Inquiry that estimates of the likely demand for water put forward by the Authority and the water undertakings were too high. He thought they were the 'best possible'. He further said that there was no assurance that any alternative source of water, such as desalination or barrages, would be available by the late seventies or afterwards at competitive rates.

'In view of the probability that another regulating

reservoir for the Severn will be judged necessary in time for the late 1970s, I consider that any promising site should be investigated in readiness for the possible promotion of a project in 1971. I conclude that the case for investigations has not been justified against all alternatives, and that because of the consequences for agriculture and particularly for the community, the use of the Dulas Valley for the next regulating reservoir in the River Severn will not be authorised.'

WESTERN MAIL

Wednesday, December 2, 1970   THE NATIONAL NEWSPAPER OF WALES   No. 31,543

Thomas stops river authority from making checks on sit

Valley freed from reservoir threat

By GERAINT TALFAN DAVIES, Our Welsh Affairs Correspondent

PLANS TO investigate sites in the Dulas Valley for a reservoir were rejected yesterday by the Secretary of State for Wales, Mr. Peter Thomas.

His decision is regarded as a major victory over Whitehall.

The Severn River Authority's application for compulsory powers to make site investigations in the valley was refused by Mr. Thomas because of the strength of sociological objections.

The decision was made in the face of strong opposition from the old Ministry of Housing and Local Government, now part of the Department of the Environment, which was backed by the Water Resources Board.

I understand the battle over Dulas accounts for the long delay in announcing the decision, which comes seven months after the public inquiry inspector, Mr. B. I.

ticularly for the community, the use of the Dulas Valley for the next regulating reservoir in the River Severn would not be authorised."

The decision is likely to encourage the opposition to a similar application for site investigations in the Senni Valley.

Mr. Thomas also emphasised that

He accepted the river authority would have to find additional resources in the catchment area before 1980. But no decision will be made until after the publication of a report on water resources in Wales and the Midlands which is being prepared by the Water Resources Board.

Mr. Thomas has asked the river authority to review the position in

Mr. Emlyn Hooson, Q.C., said last night the valley's victory emphasised the importance of defence committees not allowing themselves to be used by political parties.

Mr. Hooson, who represented the committee at the inquiry, said they refused the backing of any political party and fought their own case on its merits.

A spokesman for the Severn River Authority said: "The authority

nationalist claims that we control our own water res feel that the Welsh Office r than justified itself."

The M.P. for Brec Radnor, Mr. Caerwyn J said, "I welcome the deci particularly that it should been made largely on soc consideration which is wha stressing in the Senni dispute.

Happy, go-ahead community wins battle against reservoi

Dam could kill valley life, says inspector

By GERAINT TALFAN DAVIES, Our Welsh Affairs Correspondent

THE PEOPLE of the Dulas Valley form a particularly strong, virile, happy and go-ahead community which would be liable to disintegrate if a reservoir were built there.

This view was expressed by the public inquiry inspector, Mr. B. I. Brough, in his report to the Secretary of State for Wales, Mr. Peter Thomas, rejecting the application for site investigations in the Severn Valley.

Because of the likely consequences for agriculture and the community, Mr. Brough decided the next regulating reservoir on the Severn should not be built at Dulas.

But he found the drawing up of a reservoir scheme in the Severn catchment area for the late 1970s was nevertheless urgent.

Incapable

the late 1970s or afterwards at competitive rates.

"This inquiry was no place for a review of the potential of the river as now controlled," he said. "For present purposes I accept that it will probably be incapable of satisfactorily sustaining supplies expected of it by the late 1970's.

"The Water Resources Board confirm the general pattern of future demand and that deficiencies beyond acceptable risk may occur by 1978."

He added the authority would not be able to decide whether or not to promote a reservoir until after the publication next year of a report on water resources in Wales and the Midlands prepared by the Water Resources Board.

When it came to assessing alternatives, it would be helpful if a

to the present way of life and economy of the valley," said Mr. Brough. "Replacement would be perhaps by amalgamation of the severed farms to form a more mountain type of farm and by introduction of different employments and amenities which would be of interest and benefit to other people.

"The objectors can be sure that such changes, the objection that cost is not the paramount factor is fair.

Blight

"It is no part of the authority's case that the financial burden put upon consumers by the development of a more costly site would necessarily be great, but they have shown proper concern with capital cost.

"The arguments against cost

TWO TOP WRITERS ON TWO

How Dai beat a Goliath AN

KEPT HIS HEAD ABOVE WATE

THE 37 people gathered together in a classroom of a Welsh had come to celebrate a victory. After four years dogged camp they had at last succeeded in preventing their homes being floo a reservoir to supply water for the Midlands.

When this result came through, the utter relief and joy we felt was more than just palpable – it was exultation, euphoria everywhere! I was sent home from work for the rest of the day in order to take it all in. My father and Gordon Pugh were summoned to Cardiff to appear on the evening television news. Telephone calls, telegrams and letters of congratulations poured in: 'Just heard the good news, what a happy Christmas present for Dulas. The result of determined UNITED effort of course'; 'Very hearty congratulations on the wonderful news for the Dulas Valley'; 'May I congratulate you and your supporters on winning your fight to save the Dulas Valley from being drowned. In future, the name of the Dulas Valley and the way you and your people fought will be an inspiration to other Welsh Valleys similarly threatened.'

The decision was described as a 'major victory over Whitehall'. The strength of the sociological objections had triumphed. In the *Western Mail*, Geraint Talfan Davies wrote that the decision would give hope to the Senni Valley objectors. But the Secretary of State, Peter Thomas, asserted that Wales must play a full part in meeting the demand for water, which was likely to double in Britain over the next thirty years. He promised however that a full cost – benefit study would in future be absolutely necessary, taking into account all the social costs.

According to another newspaper, the Severn River Authority described the decision as '. . . a terrible set back to our plans'. The reporter continued, 'It is understood that the Authority was banking on acceptance of the Dulas proposals. It is believed it spent in the region of £100,000, much more than usual, in investigating the Valley's possibilities.'

Tribute was paid by Emlyn Hooson to the Defence Committee. The members had not allowed themselves to be used by political parties and had fought their own case on its merits. The decision was said to have rocked the House of Commons and was indeed warmly welcomed by MPs on all sides . . . Caerwyn Roderick, then the MP for Brecon and Radnor, welcomed the fact that the decision had been made largely on sociological considerations, as they had been stressing these factors in the Senni Valley. Gwynfor Evans, President of Plaid Cymru, thought it was good that the Government had refused to allow 'this evil' and had regard for the interest and opinion of Wales. 'In any other country,' he added, 'this would have been taken for granted.' The NFU described the result as a great victory for common sense – it was the first time that an application of this nature under the Water Resources Act had been refused by a Minister.

On the day the result was declared, Gordon Pugh said, 'We have done no work on the farm today – everybody's in such a whirl. There will be a celebration and probably a service of thanksgiving.' My father commented, 'There is a great feeling of relief, as if a great cloud which has hung over the Valley for years, has disappeared.' Gareth Morgan was equally moved: 'I think it shows you have to be united. The Dulas people had a good case and they pursued it relentlessly. It is also clear you can't do it on your own, you must have expert advice. You must also have money. It cost £1,500 to employ me and a junior barrister at the Inquiry. If Emlyn Hooson had charged a fee, he could have asked for £3,000. It is grossly unfair that this financial burden should rest entirely on the objectors in a Public Inquiry. I think some form of legal aid should be granted.'

It was summed up generously and accurately by an article in The *British Weekly*:

'Never has interest flagged on the issue of Welsh Water, but never perhaps has it risen so high as when there was a Public Inquiry into the Severn River Authority's request that the Secretary of State should make an order permitting them to carry out trial borings with a view to constructing a dam and regulating reservoir in the Dulas Valley. The case is of more than local interest because large issues are involved. In particular, there is the all-important consideration in what proportion you must weigh the economic and sociological factors. There can be no doubt that after possible sites had been reduced to ten in number, two sites in the Dulas Valley were recommended by the consultants for trial borings. They obviously did so because they felt that this area was most suitable for their purpose. Nevertheless it seems obvious that they did not consider any sort of preliminary sociological survey. One of the partners of the firm which carried out the survey even declared that "By the very nature of the Valley spurs and the division of the Valley between the counties of Radnorshire and Montgomeryshire it is a somewhat divided community." This statement rested on no sort of research and was later shown to be completely without foundation. The report went on to say, "The local objectors therefore did a public service. They stood four square on their elementary rights, they brought in experts to adduce, on the basis of sound research, that there was an economically viable community with a rich community life. The plain man and the expert need not necessarily be at loggerheads, but it is always necessary that people should not be overawed by officialdom. The case therefore, is of immediate interest to us all. One must never under estimate these community links just because they cannot be evaluated in cost-benefit terms. There can be no doubt that although Professor Carter and Mr Lewis

(Aberystwyth University) approached their task objectively, they did come, as a result of their investigations, to the conclusion that a society that has been built up over very many generations should not be destroyed." '

That view was echoed by a Mr Thayer in his article in The *Local Government Chronicle*, who gave high marks for the fact that the Dulas Valley Defence Committee sought a survey of demographic and community characteristics. In its conclusion, its authors claimed that the local view in Montgomeryshire that this was a distinctive area with its own marked feeling, was fully substantiated. Mr Thayer continued:

'There are certain issues arising from this investigation that will need to be considered when future reservoir sites are planned. The disposition is always to suppose that when people make a fuss about the flooding of their land, they are being unnecessarily awkward. The outsider who knows nothing of the past history or present conditions of the community occupying the Valley might well suppose that they obtrude their private interests, and strive therefore to obstruct the larger good. But this is not the case. It is always necessary to be on one's guard against the undue assertions of power from above, even when it is acting in the public interest and for the public good. Democracy will be whittled away and local feeling discounted if, too easily, the expert is allowed to have his own way. This is underlined when, in the case of the Dulas Valley, the expert had obviously only noticed those factors that concern his immediate project and has not taken sufficient account of sociological factors, which, in plain terms, means the human conditions in which the people live. The Dulas Valley highlights all such cases because it underlines the truth that only when you have a complete survey of all the known factors, can you come to a proper conclusion. Therefore there emerged a fascinating picture of a dispute in which there is not just the cut and thrust of counter-argument, but the lives of men and women.'

The Senni Valley people were going through the same trauma as ourselves, but their fight differed from ours. They were fighting the Usk River Authority, who wanted water for Wales – Cardiff, in fact. They were arguing as we had, on the grounds of preserving their culture, the beauty of the landscape, the quality of the farming and their way of life. The flooding of Welsh valleys was a very topical and emotive subject. Welsh extremists were very active and explosions had been a fairly regular occurrence. A spokesman for the Senni said that in the light of the result of the Dulas Inquiry, the Secretary of State would be asked immediately to call a halt to the planned borings. It would be a contradiction to grant a reprieve in one case and not in the other. 'Senni,' he said, 'is equally as virile a community as Dulas.'

The *Western Mail* concluded:
> 'So far only Dulas knows its fate, and a happy one it is. The Dulas decision will be accepted as setting some pretty popular precedents. One can hope for Senni, but only weep for Tryweryn which was forced to fight its battle a decade too soon, before conservation, cost-benefit analysis and even before the days of a Secretary of State for Wales, the Principality's new final arbiter in latest Government mythology.'

On 28 October 1971, the Water Resources Board

published its report on the Senni. It opposed the drowning of the Valley and said that the necessary extra water could be got largely by redeveloping existing reservoirs. Mr Glyn Powell, the leading twenty-nine-year-old activist and Secretary of the Senni Defence Committee, said that the decision not to drown the Dulas Valley had been important. '. . . But all we wanted was to show that there was no need to drown the Senni. The Committee had got experts to do studies to show how the projected water needs might otherwise be met. We've done that.'

The Senni too was saved.

My reaction the day the result was announced

It was a cold December morning when, along with my sister Hilary, I braved the harsh weather to set out for work. We had been spared the usual trek across fields to catch the service bus as, on that day, our father had told us we could borrow his car.

Having parked up in Llanidloes, I made my way to the office and Hilary to the Milk Bar next door, where she worked. I felt rather weary as I began to open the morning mail. Maybe I'd been late to bed the night before, or perhaps I was going down with something. Suddenly I came across an envelope which for some reason stood out from the others. I can't remember why, but almost instinctively I opened it. What I saw didn't register immediately, but on reading it a second time, I could feel my heart beat faster – and then it hit me! There, before my very eyes, was the news that we had all been patiently awaiting with bated breath. I was having difficulty taking it in.

It was a letter notifying that the Inspector, Brian Brough, had come down in our favour, citing amongst other things that our community and way of life were simply too precious to be destroyed. There was to be no reservoir in the Dulas Valley!

Had he been in the room, I would have undoubtedly given him a great big hug. Whilst it was not my place to do so, I felt the very least I could do would be to give him a call to express our gratitude, sheer joy and relief at his conclusion. I struggled to conceal my tears so as not to feel embarrassed in front of colleagues, but I needn't have worried. As the news broke, the entire office became overcome with euphoria, as one colleague after another entered the room. Incredulity soon gave way to celebration and a bottle of Champagne appeared as if by magic.

The telephone began ringing and seemed not to stop as the news spread throughout the community and beyond. Then my father called to say that he needed the car urgently. He had received an invitation from a television channel to travel down to Cardiff immediately with Gordon Pugh to appear that evening. They couldn't waste any time as Cardiff was, at that time, a two and a half hours' drive away.

'But Dad' I protested, 'we are in the middle of celebrating, but I suppose as it's so important I'll ask if I can be excused.' After a couple of glasses of bubbly, my seniors were only too happy to release me for the rest of the day. It was after all a landmark occasion!

I set off for home at some speed, feeling on top of the world. It seemed a long six miles. My mother, having been anxiously scanning the only part of the road that could be seen from the house, came rushing out. She asked why the car had its lights switched on. I must have inadvertently switched them on in my excitement, or there again, perhaps that glass of Champagne had gone to my head? I'll never know, but in any event news like that doesn't happen every day!

It was a morning that will be etched into my memory until I draw my last breath.

Marian Harris

Chapter Ten

Celebrations

After the dust had settled, there was a gathering in our local primary school at Nantgwyn. We had been through a very trying number of years and the successful outcome deserved some sort of recognition. This was a meeting to discuss what sort of celebration we should have.

The consensus was that we should hold a Service of Thanksgiving, as Gordon Pugh had earlier suggested. There could have been other forms of celebration but this seemed more appropriate. When the dark clouds had gathered, we had been given strength and guidance through our doubts and uncertainties to reach this successful conclusion. There were then long discussions on the date and the venue and form of the service. Should we get someone famous as a guest speaker? Was the Llanidloes Community Centre suitable, where the Inquiry had been held? There were great deliberations, but we decided eventually that we would hold the service in the heart of the community, in Nantgwyn Baptist Chapel. It was the largest of the chapels and could seat the most people. Anyone could come. We were not going to restrict numbers by invitation only, although we would invite our legal team and those who had taken part in other capacities in the Inquiry.

It was the middle of the Christmas Celebrations and the members of the Young Farmers' Club were trying to fit in the popular annual round of carol singing for charity. But everyone turned out to celebrate. On 16 December, the chapel was full to capacity. The service was conducted by the Rev. T. J. Williams. Prayers were said by John Davies of Garthfawr, representing Beulah; Edward Bound of Cefn, (Cwmbelan); Oswald Woosnam (Newchapel); Iorwerth Evans (Sychnant); and Gordon Pugh (Nantgwyn). Colonel W. S. Hough read the scripture lesson and short addresses were delivered by the Reverends John Pugh, Hefin Williams and T. J. Williams himself. The most memorable moment was when the Rev. T. J. Willliams described his impression of the Inquiry. 'There were fine speeches indeed,' he said, and referred specifically to the picture of a dead and drowned valley from the closing address of Martin Thomas. But for him, the finest and most emotional moment, which demonstrated the true and generous spirit of the Dulas, was the spontaneous applause which was given to the River Authority's counsel, Michael Mann, at the close of his address. The service was

NANTGWYN CHAPEL PANTYDWR

A Thanksgiving Service

held at the above Chapel

on Wednesday, 16th December, 1970

at 7.30 p.m. by the inhabitants of the Dulas Valley

to celebrate the welcome announcement

by the Secretary of State that no reservoir

would be constructed in the valley

Officers of The Dulas Valley Defence Committee
Mr. T. I. EVANS, Chairman
Mr. G. P. PUGH, Secretary
Mr. J. PRICE, Treasurer

Please keep this leaflet as a memento of the occasion

*Gareth Morgan (Solicitor), Emlyn Hooson QC MP (Counsel),
Iorwerth Evans and Gordon Pugh*

a fitting tribute to the arduous, traumatic and highly
charged campaign we had waged.

At a further celebration in the New Year, a presentation
was made to Emlyn Hooson as a mark of our indebtedness
to him for his generosity and for the part he had played in
saving our homes and livelihoods.

Many years have passed but, on reflection, the Dulas
was a battlefield on which we demonstrated that the values
of home, culture and way of life must still be paramount.
This is a world where the power of authority supported by
number-crunching statistics can increasingly dominate
unless it is challenged. Someone mightier than us was
looking after our interests. At times I wonder whether the
spirit of Owain Glyndŵr, who knew the Valley well, saw
our predicament as evidence of the continuing subjugation
of his country. No doubt he would have rejoiced to see us
triumph. Ultimately he faltered and no one knows his last

resting place. Just as he faded away into obscurity, so our valley and all the life within it could have disappeared from memory.

Forty years after the deadline predicted for water shortages, no other Welsh valley has been lost to water. The control of water resources is passing to our own Welsh Assembly Government in Cardiff. Nature renews itself and adapts to imbalances caused by the interventions of man. There are fewer curlews and other ground nesting birds than there used to be. But red kites, unknown at the time of the Inquiry, are now here in abundance as are polecats, once rare. We still see dippers in the river, and there are lambs in the fields in the spring, primroses in the hedgerows and later, bluebells throughout the woods. Farming remains the bedrock, though there are periodical challenges and change. There are new people in the Valley, incomers who enrich our community further, as they have over the centuries. But the Dulas endures.

Recollections – Martin Thomas

When I am travelling through from South Wales to my home in Gresford in the North, I occasionally take the time to travel the road over from Rhayader to Llanidloes so that I can see the Dulas Valley once again. I do so with some satisfaction and with some pride that I played a small part in saving this green and rolling countryside from the devastation that threatened in 1970. It is a beautiful part of Wales and, as I found out, lived and worked in by delightful people.

When I became involved, the proposals by the Severn Water Authority were well advanced – so was the opposition roused by the Dulas Defence Committee and its excellent and committed leaders, Iorwerth Evans, Gordon Pugh and others. They had already decided upon their policy: no protests, no demonstrations – particularly political demonstrations. They were to win on the strength and values of the community and the economic arguments against the waste of good agricultural land and the farming skills that went with it.

I had been at the Bar in Chester for some three years but was already involved in the political life of Wales, having fought the two general elections of 1964 and 1966 in West Flintshire as a Liberal. The drowning of Welsh valleys to provide water resources for the large conurbations in England was, following Tryweryn, a hot political issue, marked by the explosions and the arson which threatened the harmony and concord of daily life in North and Mid Wales. But my firm instructions were to avoid the politics, and to concentrate on the case.

Gareth Morgan, the genial and highly talented solicitor from Llanidloes, co-ordinated and directed operations. It was a stroke of genius to involve the Geography department of the University of Wales, Aberystwyth, with its two principals, Gregynog Professor Harold Carter and Senior Lecturer Roy Lewis. Their Report, 'A Survey of Demographic and Community Characteristics', underpinned the evidence presented to the Inspector by the residents of the Valley. It provided the proof, if proof were needed, of the structural links which bound the Valley together and gave it a greater cohesion and mutual support than any urban community which had been subject to similar analysis.

I have three abiding memories of the Inquiry. First, the concert in the Llanidloes Community Centre the night before the Inquiry commenced: there was such talent on stage, entirely from the Valley. Spirits were lifted even though the fatal day had almost dawned. The only regret was that the Inspector and our opposing team of lawyers had decided that it was inappropriate to attend. My second memory is of tears, of turning around at the end of my closing speech and seeing that many of the audience were weeping. My third is of applause: applause for Michael Mann QC when he had concluded his final address on behalf of the Severn River Authority. If anything demonstrated the generosity of spirit of the people it was that: they were prepared to clap him for his professionalism in the presentation of his case day after day, in the presence of hundreds who deeply opposed the purposes of his clients. It was unsurprising that at the celebratory service held in Nantgwyn Baptist Chapel following the successful result of the Inquiry, the Reverend T. J. Williams singled that applause out as the most outstanding moment of the proceedings.

I am so grateful to Marian for bringing it all back to me. Searching around in the loft at home, I came across my notebook of the evidence and speeches and Marian has kindly incorporated my notes as an Appendix to her very full recollection of these stirring and memorable events.

Martin Thomas
May 2018

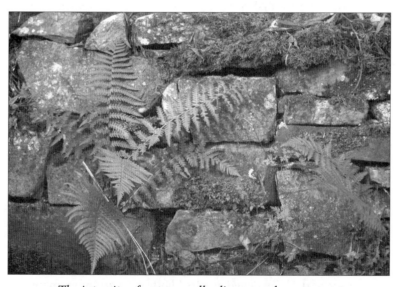

The integrity of a stone wall relies on each component supporting its neighbour, a strategy mimicked by local inhabitants in order to preserve their own integrity and way of life. Country dwellers learn a great deal from their forebears, who were blessed with reasoning and common sense. The world constantly moves on, but there are times when we would be well advised to look back in order to learn.

Recollections – Gordon Pugh

I have to say that, at my advanced age, things don't come so easily to mind as they once did... things get a little clouded. I will, however, try to recall those occurrences which, due to their significance, still stand out clearly.

They were very testing times for all of the twenty nine sites in Mid Wales that were the subject of investigations, but particularly for our community in the Dulas Valley which was eventually singled out as the preferred choice of the Severn River Authority. I believe that cost considerations were a prime factor in their decision, rather than concern for the large number of people who would have been affected.

We decided amongst ourselves that we had to fight to save our community and everything that it stood for. A defence committee was formed for the Dulas Valley with Iorwerth Evans ('Iory' to me) as Chair, myself as Secretary, John Price as Treasurer and representatives from the properties involved. Collectively, we would all do our very best to stave off this very serious threat.

Iory and I journeyed up to Llanfair Caereinion many times to attend the Mid Wales (Reservoirs) Defence Committee meetings, where we were able to have our say. The Chairman of the Severn River Authority at the time was a little terrier, but he was to have a difficult time at any meetings that he attended.

On one particularly rough winter's night, there had been a bad snowstorm and I was unable to drive down our lane to reach the main road in Pantydwr. Luckily, Emrys Evans (Green Farm) was able to get his van out and we somehow managed to reach Llanfair – no easy feat given the conditions.

Whenever we held a meeting of the Dulas Valley Defence Committee, Mansel Jones, a reporter for the Western Mail, would come up to find out what had gone on. I remember being interviewed several times by BBC Wales who would then send a cheque through the post because they wanted to reserve the right to have those interviews. If I remember rightly, I would give that money to the Dulas Defence Committee fighting fund.

We had decided to approach our task in a professional manner even though the threat of people coming onto our land for investigative purposes was hard to bear. A police sergeant said that if the Authority's staff or their agents were trespassing on our land, we could not in law turn them off as private property counts for nothing in the end. When I asked him if I could stop them coming through the gate, his reply was that I couldn't. In that event I think there was an arrangement about letting each other know if anyone was seen to be doing this, but I can't be sure of the mechanics. I have a feeling that it would have been no more than agreed telephone contact and nothing more complicated than that.

There was so much involvement that it is difficult for me to remember a lot of what went on. I was a young man at the time and had a great deal of respect for Iory Evans. We got on very well.

I do have vivid recollections of the Public Inquiry where we all gave our statement. Martin Thomas acted very well on our behalf and the hall was packed every day.

When the result came down in our favour, it was a tremendous feeling. It was such a relief that we could all now see the way ahead and still have a future. The uncertainty had gone and we would still have our homes. Any compensation would, in comparison, have been negligible. Our determination to stop the proposals gaining approval was undoubtedly down to our bonding together for the sake of our way of life. I am so thankful that it never came about and that we still have a vibrant community where there is still a lot going on.

On the day it was announced, Iory and I were invited down to Cardiff to be interviewed by the BBC. We had to 'down tools' and rush down there at short notice, but it was worth it. Some time later Iory and I were asked to speak about our experiences at the annual dinner of the Llanidloes branch of the NFU.

More recently, whilst visiting a friend in Llanidloes, we decided to call on the late Lady Hooson, wife of the late Emlyn Hooson QC who had very kindly waived his fee for acting on our behalf. Whilst there I was invited to see the impressive collection of The Works of William Shakespeare, which from memory comprised some eight volumes. They had been presented to Lord Hooson by the people of the Dulas Valley as an expression of gratitude for his help and generosity. We spent a very pleasant time chatting.

This area of Mid Wales is very special. Our victory is merely a reflection of the way in which we as residents felt about living here.

Gordon Pugh

Recollections –
Mansel Jones

My over-riding memory of the campaign to save the Dulas Valley and of the subsequent Public Inquiry was of the friendly way in which both had been conducted. In my *Western Mail* report of the final day of the Inquiry at Llanidloes I wrote: 'The friendly atmosphere of the Inquiry was maintained to the end.'

On the last day the final speeches by all main speakers, including that of Mr Michael Mann, representing the Severn River Authority, were applauded by everyone in the packed hall.

However, had the Welsh Office decision gone differently in the end, things would probably not have remained friendly. On Day 7, Mr Iorwerth Evans, Chair of the Defence Committee, promised 'a David and Goliath of a fight' if the River Authority had been allowed to start test drillings.

As the *Western Mail's* reporter in the area I always found both Mr Iorwerth Evans and the defence committee secretary, Mr Gordon Pugh, ready and willing to answer questions and provide background help.

The Dulas Valley Defence Committee ran a quiet, methodical campaign. They assiduously avoided antagonising the political parties, even refusing help from Plaid Cymru. Plaid, nevertheless, appeared at the Inquiry on their own behalf. Even without the political parties, the committee fielded an impressive array of objectors and were even astute enough to engage an expert engineer from Salford University to support their case.

On a personal level, staying at the Red Lion in Llanidloes with the other Press corps covering the Inquiry wasn't always easy as the Chairman of the Inquiry, Mr Brian Brough, was staying at the same small hotel. Journalists don't always get a good name but we all made sure Mr Brough had his privacy.

I celebrated my 24th birthday at the Inquiry and it was just about the last story I covered for the *Western Mail* first time around as I left in March 1970 to become press officer of the Wales Tourist Board. I later returned to the *Western Mail* in Swansea and later in Cardiff.

Mansel Jones
June 2018

This tree in an exposed position above the valley was torn asunder by the elements, but the winds of change failed to destroy our community, which defied all odds to win the day.

Acknowledgements

Immeasurable thanks to Martin Thomas OBE, QC (*Lord Thomas of Gresford*), for discussing the idea with me in the first instance, thereby sharing my enthusiasm and reasons for documenting the events of that time. Also for his valued help in redacting the draft and contributing his recollections and factual addendum.

Councillor Gareth Morgan LL B – my then employer – for progressing the idea with me following our success.

Rev Dr John Morgans for convincing me that the story was one worth telling and for inspiring the confidence to see it through.

Myrddin ap Dafydd for his support and enthusiasm for the project, without which the book might not have materialised.

Friends and members of my family who encouraged me along the way.

My niece-in-law Fflur Davies (*nee Pughe*) for her guidance with regard to publication and to Jane Burnard for proof-reading the draft.

Gordon Pugh for his recollections of involvement on the Defence Committee.

Mansel Jones of The Western Mail for his reminiscences of the unfolding events.

Finally to my husband Vyvyan for his enormous contribution to the book, particularly in terms of research, for his unfailing patience and support throughout the project, his help in initial editing – and for photographing our extant valley.

I have tried my best to recall the facts and all those who were involved with events as they unfolded. In so doing, I apologise for any errors, misrepresentations or omissions that may have inadvertently occurred – fifty years is a long time!

The cooperation and steadfastness of the 'commonalty' ensured that the sun would never set on their revered way of life. They defied those who sought otherwise... and won a hard, decisive but very significant battle.

In representing residents of the Dulas Valley past and present, the author wishes to express sympathy for all those who lost their homes, livelihoods, culture and history in Capel Celyn as a result of the construction of the Tryweryn dam.

Their cataclysmic misfortune triggered a measured, determined response from our community when faced with the same prospect.

It is to be hoped that our victory has set a precedent preventing other Welsh valleys being flooded without due consideration being given to social and cultural implications.

Marian Harris

The publishers wishes to acknowledge that cuttings are included from the following newspapers in this book:

DAILY EXPRESS; Express Newspapers/N & S syndication; Editor: Natalie Jones

GUARDIAN & OBSERVER; Courtesy of Guardian News & Media Ltd.; Guardian reporter: Simon Hoggart, Observer reporters: Mary Holland and Joanne Slaughter

WESTERN MAIL; Reporters: Geraint Talfan Davies, Samuel Knight, Mansel Jones

LIVERPOOL DAILY POST; Reporters: David Lloyd and Iorwerth Roberts

THE TIMES; Reporter: Trevor Fishlock

BIRMINGHAM POST

THE COUNTY TIMES AND EXPRESS & GAZETTE; Editor: Jonny Knight

LOCAL GOVERNMENT CHRONICLE; Reporter: Richard Thayer, Editor: Nick Goulding

BRITISH WEEKLY

Martin Thomas' addendum

The Inspector emphasised in opening the Inquiry that its purpose was to examine the case for and against site investigations and not to consider whether a reservoir should be constructed in the Dulas Valley – that was a separate question. He was aware that people were seeking to introduce the wider issues and he was not disposed to object to hearing such evidence within reasonable limits. It was not irrelevant. The Secretary of State would wish to be as widely informed as possible. In answer to Emlyn Hooson, he emphasised that if evidence outside the scope of the Inquiry was heard, then provided he agreed to hear it, it would be reported on to the Secretary of State – he would not restrict the scope of the Inquiry any more than he must do.

For the River Severn Authority, Counsel said that they were not appearing as promoters and were not propounding the case for the reservoir. Mr Hooson said that it would be quite unrealistic to think that Dulas was not thought to be the site of a reservoir. It would be fooling the public if the Severn Authority did not realise this was a serious Inquiry with results that could affect the public. They must understand that the evidence the objectors would adduce was relevant as to whether large sums of public money should be spent on site investigations.

Michael Mann QC in opening his case declared that the River Severn was a major source for the supply of water. The West Midlands, Coventry, Gloucester and Bristol were dependent on abstractions from it. The Clywedog Dam began its operations on 1 April 1968 to maintain the flow of water as measured at Bewdley at 160 million gallons a day (mgd). According to estimates prepared in the late 1950s or early 60s, it would suffice until 1981.

But Clywedog would not be able to meet the need in 1978. At one time, it was feared it would fail in 1975, but by some re-allocation of resources, the overall deficiency had been postponed to 1978. It would steadily increase from that time on. The demand for water was increasing by reason of improved standards of living, changing social habits and industrial demand. The Central Advisory Water Committee had assumed that the demand for water in England and Wales would roughly double by the end of the century.

The question was how the demand was to be met. It was a question not for the Severn River Authority but for the Secretary of State and Parliament. There was no alternative but to use the Severn if the demands of the 'ten year period', the years 1978 to 1988, were to be met. It was also the view of the Water Resources Board. These demands could only be met by further regulation of the Severn.

There were many possible sites. The Welsh Advisory Committee had listed twenty-four sites in their 1961 Report: the SRA used that Report as their base when it was instructed to report on sites. Binnie and Partners proposed to look at twenty-nine sites, a number which had created alarm and had been raised in Parliament by Emlyn Hooson on 27 May 1966 when he spoke of the anxieties and fears of his constituents.

Ten valleys had been considered by Binnie and Partners with a surface exploration of public rights of way and highways but there had been no subsurface explorations.

Their task was to find a site that could accommodate a reservoir holding not less than 18,000 million gallons. This amount of regulated storage was the calculated figure, necessary if abstractors' predicted demands were to be met throughout the ten year period 1978–1988 whilst maintaining the flow at Bewdley at 160 mgd. It took into account a two per cent probability of drought – i.e one in every fifty years.

Four of the ten sites were eliminated, either because they could not hold 18,000 million gallons or the catchment area was insufficient. In most of the remaining six sites, storage could be provided to meet the demand beyond the ten-year period. Those required more detailed examination.

If a reservoir were built, Mr Mann said that the SRA appreciated that there would be considerable disruption and hardship to those who lived in the Dulas Valley, and that was regretted. But it was unavoidable if demands were to be met from the Upper Severn Catchment area. Only one of the remaining five valleys was less objectionable on social and agricultural grounds and that was the Gam Valley but the cost of developing Gam was out of all proportion to the advantages it possessed in social and agricultural terms. Regulating reservoirs, he argued, did have local advantages – flood alleviation and the provision of recreational facilities. He pointed to the schemes in valleys on the Wye.

The SRA desired to carry out detailed site examinations to prove the feasibility of various schemes which were proposed for the Dulas Valley. Drill holes were needed on the sites of possible rock fill quarrying. Clay borrow pits, borehole pits and trenches would be required at dam sites and on the line of the three aqueducts proposed. Trial embankments would be constructed to test the embanking qualities of local rock. Material for this purpose would be excavated from a small quarry in the adjacent hillside. The total operations would take four to six months to complete. At the end of that time, the SRA would reinstate holes and pits with marker pins left behind. The trial embankment would be grounded to an agreed profile and grassed.

The SRA could not obtain permission from all the landowners involved – sixty-five in all – and the application was for compulsory powers. It was strongly supported by the Water Resources Board. The application had attracted a volume of objectors – eighty-one on record. The objectors had either given no reason or base for their objections or based them simply on the undesirability of constructing a reservoir in the Dulas Valley. The planning permissions required fell within the area of two local authorities. Montgomeryshire County Council had granted permission while Radnorshire took the view that as no permanent development was sought for, permission was not required.

The proving or disproving of sites was a matter of urgency. The issue had its genesis in 1966 and the need was going to arise in 1978. Are the West Midlands and the other towns and cities, asked Mr Mann rhetorically, to have their water supplies at risk? Somebody has to decide how the demand is to be met and no one had suggested otherwise than by further regulation of the Severn. The SRA had a statutory responsibility to implement a decision and it was essential to know now whether a reservoir in the Dulas Valley was feasible.

Mr Mann ended with a flourish: 'We do not see how the Minister or the Secretary of State can take a decision, unless he knows whether the most promising site was feasible. That is why we are promoting this Order. It will be the end of a period of blight and uncertainty which has been overhanging the community for a number of years.'

Mr Haines, the Chief Engineer of the SRA, was the first witness. Emlyn Hooson QC set out to show that the Authority had not weighed the impact on the community against the technical feasibility of the site in their choice of the Dulas for their investigations. In cross examination, Mr Haines agreed that he accepted 1978 as the crucial date, but that if he was wrong about that, the urgency departed. The water had to come from the Severn basin and any sociological grounds of objection must be over ridden by technical grounds. The estimated cost of the investigation of the Dulas Valley would be £95,000 and if the site were not technically possible, the SRA would be very disappointed. The Authority had not considered it necessary to carry out a sociological survey – they were concerned with the technical features. They had commissioned a land agent to investigate land values but although they assumed there would be objection on sociological grounds, they had carried out no social evaluation themselves. He agreed, however, that there was no point in investigating the site at all if it were to be turned down because of the sociological aspects.

Mr Hooson, for the Dulas Defence Committee, questioned Mr Haines about the Clywedog project. The forecasts were that Clywedog would be needed by 1968 but its resources had not yet been used. Indeed, even after the dry summer of the previous year, the daily flow was way above anything needed. Mr Haines agreed that the SRA might never have to use the Clywedog before 1980. It would be wrong to say that everybody made perfect forecasts but if the figures were wrong in the past, the figures for the future were not necessarily wrong. Clywedog was an insurance policy. He agreed that one of the proposed 10 sites, the Upper Severn, was uninhabited and could provide 4.4 million gallons' storage as additional insurance.

Mr Haines was further questioned about the possibility of water storage in the Oswestry/Salop area. The consultants had only considered sites in the Upper Severn, nothing downstream. There had been studies into the water – bearing strata in Oswestry/Salop but not for storage. It was doubtful if there could be both extraction and storage.

The alternative scheme propounded by Dr Wilson was put to him. He agreed that it would be attractive to develop an area where there were no dwellings with the capacity four times that of the proposed Dulas scheme, more so if it were to be combined with electricity generation. Further, a plan which avoided the drowning of a valley would be desirable in the national interest. But his approach was that the development was so urgent that, 'We must have the Dulas.' The SRA were wanting to carry out site investigations because the consultants had indicated the Dulas, and 'We have done what we have been told.'

Mr Tasker Watkins VC QC entered the fray on behalf of the local authorities. In answering his questions, Mr Haines said that Tylwch, which would be drowned whichever site was adopted in the Valley, was not considered to be a village. The chances of the site being a suitable site were good, following the consultants' geological investigations. On the annual expected rate of increase in demand, he said that three per cent was the general figure across the country and although there were possibly short recessions from time to time, as in Birmingham the previous year, it was a safe assumption that demand would continue to rise to the end of the century. There were no signs of reaching peak consumption. The SRA knew of nothing which was likely to offer an alternative solution. The investigations would be over in six months and the Authority were appointing a private firm of land agents to deal with compensation claims.

In further questioning, Mr Haines contended that desalination or barrage schemes provided no answer. There was very little research going on into such matters. He could see no alternative. Questions of flood control were very important to the Authority and figured prominently with them. Flood alleviation would be a desirable side benefit.

The consulting engineer, Mr R. V. C. Phillips, was the second witness for the applicants. He pointed out that a regulating dam discharges water into the river and not into pipes. 'Demand is assessed at the abstraction point according to the flow of the river. All daily flows are computed and there is a lengthy calculation working on a daily basis as to what the flow will be and what amount it is necessary to release from the reservoir to make up the flow at the abstraction point. There is a considerable lag between the release of water from the reservoir and its arrival at the abstraction point. It took two to five days for water to flow from Clywedog to Bewdley. A certain amount of the water is lost as waste: fifteen per cent is the assessment in our case. That is an arguable figure and may be on the low side since Clywedog is a young development and it has not been established what is a safe figure. If the flow is maintained at Bewdley at 160 mgd, it maintains the flow of 250 mgd at Gloucester. Clywedog is not at maximum demand and even if the fifty-year drought were to occur before 1978, the water from Clywedog will not be fully utilised. But if the two per cent probable increase in demand occurs, then in 1978, in conditions of fifty-year drought, the reservoir would be empty. Clywedog is not £5 million of white elephant. The chance of using it increases year by year as demand increases, biting into the catchment. The figure of 18,000 million gallons of storage I calculate at Dulas will maintain with abstractions, the flow of 160 mgd at Bewdley, taking into account the fifteen per cent wastage allowance.'

Cross-examined by Mr Tasker Watkins, Mr Phillips said his calculations were from his computer. He had not been able to get onto the land but worked from existing plans and from past access. They were not in sufficient detail to enable him to site the dam exactly. He had a comprehensive geological map of the area which revealed three main faults. One was to the north of the lower site in an east-west direction. The second was upstream of the upper site, also in an east-west direction. The third was a fault to the south of the proposed reservoir in the vicinity of Wenallt and Ystwyth. He said, 'We are seeking to investigate these faults. They are not yet categorised and they must be clarified.' He did not know a possible site had been rejected on geological grounds – they had been allowed only to consider the ten specific sites. But he had no reservations about embarking on the investigations because he was confident they would turn out to be all right. He conceded that an adverse geological investigation might dissuade him – in particular, he agreed that the reason for a gorge, as at the northern end of the site, was usually a fault.

The costs allowed for the lower site were £375,000, and for the upper site, £157,000. The effective cost of the whole project at the date of its commissioning was £1.03 million. Roads were estimated £461,000 and land, £569,000. This included the cost of a new road from Llanidloes to Pantydwr with fresh farm accesses. The cost of a major diversion of the B-road was also included, as was the provision of an amenity road to make easy access on the east side to the lake. He had calculated some costs for the Gam site but no plans were available. The costs of storage on the Gam were high. He said that if the costs had been the same, he would have recommended the Gam for development.

Under pressure from Mr Watkins, Mr Phillips conceded that his choice of the Dulas had been weighted only by the factor of money – subject only to the findings of the investigations. He had not considered a contest between sociological factors, agricultural disturbance and the higher cost of the Gam scheme. He agreed that the whole exercise was being conducted on the basis of the SRA's calculation of the increase in demand. But he insisted that the Clywedog Dam, though not at that point in time having been brought fully into play, remained always useful and would be so even if empty and out of use, since as soon as it started to refill use could be made of it. When asked by Mr Tasker Watkins if it had ever been empty, he replied that at varying times it had only been half full: 'The demand for water has to be met from somewhere.' Mr Watkins suggested there had to be a coincidence of two speculative things – a unique drought and a build up of demand. Mr Phillips agreed that unless there was an extraordinary coincidence, the Clywedog could perform its role for years after 1978. But bigger droughts might happen within seven years and there might be a failure of the design yield.

As for desalination, Mr Phillips said that the process was growing abroad fairly rapidly where there was no other alternative. It had first been contemplated in the South-east of England where water was getting more and more expensive and scarce. There it was used in conjunction with other sources. It would compare with other costs of getting water, for example, for consumers close to the desalination plant. But where water was cheap and consumers were a long way from the sea, it would not be viable. Bristol took a substantial amount of water from the Severn but there were no plans for desalination plants in the next ten years: it was a matter of cost and it might come in the future.

The next cheapest site to Dulas was the Gam where there would be less agricultural damage and fewer people would be displaced but the estimated cost would be £1.4 million. The disparity of cost between Dulas and Gam arose out of the requirement for far greater quantities of fill for the suggested Gam dam. Mr Phillips explained that they had found five sites which would not flood any houses and eleven possible sites where no more than three houses would be lost. But all those areas were rejected because desk studies showed that there were high cost and engineering problems. A combination of two or more of these sites would provide sufficient water for future need but cost and operational control made this solution unviable.

Mr Phillips offered assurances to the people of Pantydwr. The proposed works would not eliminate the hamlet. Diversions would be underground, and pipelines so arranged as to go in the most convenient place. The pipelines might join and have a common outlet. There would be no more than temporary disturbance to the fields through which the pipelines would run. There was no reason why there should be any great disturbance. As for the central and lower parts of the site where there would be a considerable number of boreholes involving several farms, the land would be freed after three months, the soil replaced on top and the area vacated. He could not say how long it would take to restore the land to pasturage.

Mr Hooson took up the cudgels and challenged the forecast figures. The witness agreed that much depended on their accuracy. If there was a margin of error, the time scale would be altered. Mr Phillips had compared actual flows with forecast flows for Clywedog and accepted that they were less than forecast and that the Bewdley gauge figures were inaccurate because the bed of the river had altered.

As for Dr Wilson's plan, Mr Phillips had not investigated the Cefn Brwyn site but even so, he thought it very much more expensive and wondered whether, with an eight-year refill period, it would fill up at all. As for combining it with electricity generation, he considered that thermal degradation could be a serious objection.

Mr Hooson questioned him about flood alleviation but the witness was unable to say what flood prevention provisions there would be. There were three possible options, including the early release of water from the Clywedog and the proposed Dulas reservoirs on which he had been asked to advise, but he had made no decision. He had never been asked to consider groundwater elsewhere in the county.

To Mr Patrick Freeman, appearing on behalf of the Montgomeryshire County Council, Mr Phillips said he would recommend the largest scheme in the Dulas Valley. The difference in cost between the ultimate development of the Gam and the Dulas was £1.7 million and that was a significant difference. Mr Phil Williams, representing Plaid Cymru, pointed out that the difference amounted to only 2d per household per month. The witness said he recommended the cheapest system.

In re-examination by Mr Mann, Mr Phillips said on the geological point that they had consulted all the records at the Institute of Geological Sciences, including two papers on the Ystwyth/Wenallt fault by W. V. O. Jones. The geologists had concluded that the faults were not active and there was no presently known reason why they should not be sealed if necessary. As for the Clywedog, if demand forecasts were reached and the two per cent probability of drought occurred, then it would be empty in 1978/79. The risk of failure increased with every year which passed. The Central Water Advisory Service said the demand would double between now and the end of the century and the refill period would be forty-two months – seventeen months for other head of Severn installations. As for the Cefn Brwyn alternative site, it would hold 19.7 thousand million gallons, but cost £9.42 million to build at 1968 prices.

Mr Hooson QC MP opened his case to the Inspector at this stage. He argued that there were alternatives available where there was little social cost, no community was threatened and help would be available for flood prevention. A thorough investigation should have been made on a much broader basis.

He challenged the dismissal of the Head of the River Severn site by the SRA. Nobody lived there. Most of the land was owned by the Crown and in the possession of the Forestry Commission: the trees could be harvested before a dam were built. The prospective site there would hold two thirds of the capacity of the Upper Dulas, and for a small extra cost, the catchment area could be increased by fifty per cent through side stream intakes, as on the Wye, thereby shortening the refill period from forty-two months to twenty-seven months.

In true economic cost to the community, other costs would be small. The capital cost may be more but the community cost very much less. Dr Williams had calculated the costs at 2d per family per month. But they could be less than that. If the capital costs went up by one twentieth, the overall costs would go up by one fiftieth.

The Defence Committee believed that the time had come when water consumers of the West Midlands and public bodies had become reconciled to the view that they must pay marginally more for water to ensure that no community in Mid Wales is destroyed. 'How galling it is when they read of sites being rejected for their beauty or for the preservation of rare plants. All these values are relative: set them against the value of a rich community life. Here, an alternative way of getting water exists in non-inhabited valleys. Why should it be tolerated that communities should be destroyed when it would cost consumers a matter of pence per month?'

The proposition which the objectors put forward at Cefn Brwyn as an alternative site was for a multi-purpose reservoir in an area of catchment for the River Wye. It would be not only a storage and regulating reservoir, but also would be designed to produce electricity by pump storage. Ffestiniog produced £45 per kilowatt of installed capacity at 360 MW and Cruachan £42 per kilowatt of installed capacity at 400 MW. The proposed Cefn Brwyn reservoir could produce 1,000 MW at the same rate as Ffestiniog. While the Dulas proposal made 6,473 million cubic feet of water storage available for the Severn, Cefn Brwyn would make 8,500 million cubic feet available for the Wye. Cefn Brwyn could be constructed for £35 million. It would be quite wrong to reject this scheme.

For what was government policy? On 8 November 1969 Denis Howell, the Minister of Housing and Local Government, had said that the Government would always consider a combined scheme of water storage and the generation of electricity. It was avowed Government policy. But how many combined schemes had been considered by the Central Electricity Generating Board or the Water Resources Board? We should investigate what has been done and where such consultation is taking place, he said.

Mr Hooson came to the conclusion of his argument. This was a community struggling for its very life. The scheme was unnecessary and would never have been imposed upon them if the investigation had been of a broader spectrum. All had been entirely compartmentalised. The bureaucratic machine ground on while the people had only limited authority to protest. Only in the Inquiry could the whole problem be looked at broadly. This was not obstinacy on the part of the protestors. The scheme had reached a point of development where they were faced with a choice between the human price and the economic price. It amounted to a couple of pence per month on the price of water. There was no doubt that that economic price should be paid.

For the Water Resources Board, their representative Mr Rowntree said that the Welsh Committee had looked at the proposal and two members had expressed reservations in proceeding with the investigations. The Board regretted the delay because it had endangered the possibility of investigations during the summer.

Mr Mann QC, for the proposers of the scheme, at this point made a concession: if credit were given for water going into the Severn as effluent, arising from other water sources such as boreholes, the position did not become critical until 1980. The gauge flows at Stourport did take such effluent in calculating mgd.

Submissions were then made on behalf of the South Staffordshire Water Board which supplied 200,000 mgd to Staffordshire and 800,000 mgd to Birmingham. The Board's representative said that the abstractors in these areas amounted to one in five of the population affected and had to be considered. The water was used by those who had been drawn to the Midlands in furtherance of their economic life. The water was used for agriculture, particularly for spray irrigation. It was an unpleasant situation on both sides. Relative cost had to be taken into account together with the impact on those who have to pay. Public money also was involved. His Board were immediately affected by the proposed order. The company had not acquired any additional source of supply from anywhere else. Mr Hooson had argued that the figures were over estimated but the forecasts had been made for the purpose of their business. He said that they did not know how any scheme would be financed but his company would have to pay a substantial proportion of the cost. They would need more water. It would have to come from the Severn and it would be needed by 1978. It was a very short time to implement the scheme and decisions had to be taken well in advance. Mr James Lamont, their Deputy Engineer in Chief, was called to produce his Report and give evidence on behalf of the South Staffordshire Water Board.

For the Birmingham Corporation it was said that they had no wish to press for the scheme at too early a date or for a scheme which was too large or too costly. They would have to pay a proper share and meet prudent and warranted demands. The last occasion when demand for water was overtaking available supply, Birmingham had had to take steps to initiate new sources and then get approval afterwards. Mr Whitehead, called as a witness for Birmingham, agreed that the figures projected for the Clywedog had been overestimated by fifty per cent due to an unexpected decrease in demand and a levelling off in consumption. Part was due to a slowing down of the motor industry in 1966/67. But there was no reason to alter the long term trend. The Corporation would prefer to draw water from the Severn but not necessarily so. No one wished to disturb the Dulas Valley.

Mr Close, the Regional Engineer for the Bristol Waterworks Company, agreed that difficulty arises if you try to make projections from past trends. It was not possible to piece together enough information to do a mathematical projection as had been suggested. But estimates were usually underestimates and demand always exceeded them. It appeared that although the tide flowed up and down past the intake for his company at Gloucester, salt water never reached the pumping station. At times, they needed to augment the canal at Gloucester by pumping water into it at a rate of 25 mgd. They did not take water out of it.

The spokesman for the CEGB was Mr Wilkinson, who fully admitted that the stated demand for water in 1978 was purely speculative. But the Board wanted to know if and when regulating storage would be in place. The pattern of development should show orderly and sensible progressions. The quickest solution for them would be for the investigations to take place followed by implementation of the scheme. As for the Cefn Brwyn proposal, it was his department's responsibility to recommend action. The Board was interested in pump storage schemes but he was not satisfied that the proposed site was of the right type. The disadvantages were first that it would cost £15 million more than the target figure because the hydraulic head was only 400 feet above sea level and the reservoir would be three and a half miles from the generating plant as opposed to the desired one mile. It would be less economic than at Rheidol since for every 1,000 gallons pumped, three units of electricity would be lost. Further, if Cefn Brwyn were ever drawn down to zero, it would require two years to be refilled and it would be unable to use water while sixty-five per cent of the pump storage capacity would be lost. There would therefore be no benefit if water was pumped up and lost but the Board would have to pay compensation for loss of power and the cost of pumping. Cefn Brwyn was not an economic proposition for them and hardly economic for the SRA.

Mr R. V. C. Phillips, the consulting engineer for the Severn River Authority, was re-called to deal with some of the issues which had arisen. He set out the method of his calculations of the net demand for water. He had based his calculations of design drought on the flows recorded at the Bewdley Gauge, which included effluent from other sources, or 'returned water'. These calculations were drawn from 1933 data but it would be lengthy and difficult to try to assess what differences there had been since. All he could concede was that there had been some increment. Cost comparisons with other sites were equally difficult. Presenting costs in pence per thousand gallons might be helpful but it was not the way a financier would look at it. He would be concerned with the cost of borrowing at the time of the commissioning of the project, discount rates and returns. The figures which had been produced were for comparison only and did not represent the money abstractors would actually pay. He agreed that the load on the ultimate consumer would be very small. When questioned by the Inspector, Mr Phillips said that the preliminary investigations of the site would give the necessary information as to whether the site was technically feasible. More information was required for design purposes.

The Member of Parliament for Brecon and Radnor, Mr Tudor Watkins, called on behalf of the Dulas Valley

Defence Committee, told the Inquiry that although at the outset he had been in favour of the application, he had changed his mind: 'I have become wiser'. He had thought that the survey proposed was merely visual – more a visual inspection than a geological survey. He had been familiar with the Valley since 1966 but he now realised that the application involved a great deal more disturbance than he had thought.

The statements of other witnesses for the Defence Committee were then presented to the Inspector. These included Mr Thomas Iorwerth Evans, Mr Gordon Pugh, Mr David Jones and the Reverend D. Tudor Jones. They each spoke of the strength of the community and the devastation to the life of the Valley that the proposals represented.

Dr Wilson, the Committee's expert, said that he had done some work on the Dovey Valley project and the Morecombe Bay Study but estuary schemes threw up different types of problems.

His proposed Cefn Brwyn Scheme would accommodate 50,000 mgd for a long time. But the project would not be feasible without the involvement of the CEGB. The current proposal before the Inspector was useless for its purposes. While being questioned on behalf of the CEGB about the figures he had produced, Dr Wilson said, 'Perhaps a time will come when human suffering and displacement will be placed before mere money – when that time comes, there will be no more Dulas Valley Inquiries.'

Dr Wilson had been involved in two previous Section 67 Inquiries – the Usk and the Ouse-Essex schemes. In both cases, the Minister had given permission to the applicants to go ahead – though at Usk, the applicants did not get what they wanted. The Dulas Valley, he said, is not on all fours with either the Essex Water Transfer Scheme or the Usk. The fact that the only two Inquiries which had taken place had resulted in permission being granted could not be used as a precedent. The agricultural decisions at Great Bradley in Essex had been very different. They had had very little time to find alternatives. At Dulas, the River Authority were suggesting that the crucial year was six years ahead and Mr Phillips had given evidence that the reservoir would take three years to build. There was time to think again. The Water Board had not in this case issued a warning similar to those in the two other schemes.

Nothing at the previous Inquiries, argued Dr Wilson, assisted materially with the decision here, but he was concerned lest permission to go ahead might be given, against the evidence, but merely because two previous investigations had been allowed. Any decision at Dulas would affect water policy throughout the region. 'There must be circumstances,' he said, 'in which it is right for site investigations to be refused.' Those circumstances would be:

  (a) If the disadvantages outweighed the advantages to a material degree: this involved a consideration of the degree of need and the timing for such need;

  (b) If a scheme outside the jurisdiction of the Severn River Authority can be found with less undesirable effects;

  (c) If another scheme inside the area can be found to work comparably but with less undesirable effects.

At Dulas, the agricultural disadvantages were substantial and the SRA had produced insufficient agricultural information. The Defence Committee would support programmes of desalination, extraction of underground water or a reservoir in non-agricultural land. They were not interested in the prospect of any other site in any other part of the SRA's jurisdiction. But what was required was not the weighing up of one person's expertise in isolation from that of others. The problem should be looked at as a whole: there should be full exploitation of all water resources available. There should be a single comprehensive approach.

The Report which the Defence Committee had commissioned from Professor Harold Carter and Mr Colin Roy Lewis of the University College of Wales, Aberystwyth, was presented by Mr Lewis. It was a full and thorough exposition of the social and community links of the Dulas Valley and it undoubtedly had a major effect upon the Inspector's ultimate findings. [See *Dulas Valley: A Survey of Demographic and Community Characteristics: Carter & Lewis Powys* County Archives Office, Ref: GB 0223 P/X/39]. Mr Lewis pointed out that the environment had both physical and social elements. 'You cannot alter one without an impact on the other.' The SRA had presented a blinkered approach but the high walls had to be broken down and the relevance of both elements to the proposals revealed. There were, he said, competing priorities for capital expenditure to be considered. But he had no wish to sell water to England.

At the conclusion of the evidence, the Inspector permitted Martin Thomas, junior counsel to both Tasker Watkins QC and Emlyn Hooson QC, to make a separate submission since he had been present throughout the Inquiry and had held the fort in the absence from time to time of his Leaders.

Mr Thomas said that the SRA had put four propositions before the Inquiry:
   (a)   The Authority must have 18,000 mg storage for the decade 1978–88;

(b) Technically, the Dulas Valley is the most promising site;

(c) The choice is weighted only by the factor of money;

(d) By reason of the factor of money, disruption and hardship to the community and the devastation of its economic life was inevitable.

Mr Thomas paid tribute to the elegant but sympathetic presentation of the Authority's case by Mr Michael Mann, but what lay behind these four propositions was the ugly question:

'How much is a living community worth in cash?

'Let me say categorically and unequivocally,' he continued. 'We have reached a point in time when that question cannot and should not be asked at all. Historically, we have witnessed the drowning of many valleys – not only in Wales – to serve the needs of a drifting but expanding urban population. It is not just the physical environment that is altered. A humane society today appreciates that such alteration implies the destruction of the social environment as well – that complex of closely knit friendships and family relationships which preserves values of faith, of neighbourliness, of participation.

'That appreciation of the consequences inspired the Secretary of State's speech in May 1966. The people of the Dulas Valley look to the Secretary of State to stand by the pledges that he gave. If his office has a purpose, this is a major test of that purpose.'

Mr Thomas turned to the first proposition, the question of demand. The crisis year was said to be 1978. 'Where,' he asked, 'is the evidence to support the emotive language we have heard? The demand has not been proven. If there were such a demand, one would have expected a flood, a clamour of witnesses. But seven out of eleven of the current abstractors of Severn water have not bothered to turn up to this Inquiry. Birmingham told us they would be all right until 1985/6. Bristol said the position was completely uncertain.

'Only the South Staffordshire Water Authority have been present throughout the full Inquiry and have exhibited genuine concern. They have given evidence based on the Clywedog figures of 1965 – the only figures available. But their crisis talk has not been substantiated. The Clywedog figures assessed the position as requiring 79 mgd: now they claim they need 86.5 mgd. Why this increase? They have produced no evidence to support it. The evidence we have heard elsewhere is, first, that domestic demand is increasing at precisely the same rate as it has been since 1950 and secondly, that the rate of industrial expansion has been and will be the same. Indeed, their own evidence proves an actual decrease in the domestic demand and their own enquiries as to industrial expansion extend only to next year, to 1971.

'Similarly, Birmingham had made a fifty per cent error in their 1969 Clywedog estimates, claiming industrial expansion at a rate of three and a quarter per cent: since 1965, the actual rate has been one and two-thirds per cent. If they expect a sudden increase in industrial expansion, they have been unable to substantiate that expectation – they say their enquiries are not complete. Their crisis year is 1985/86.

'As for Bristol, what is their position? That is a secret locked in the heart of Bristol Waterworks. They needed some persuasion to join the Clywedog scheme, where their graphs referred to abstractions of "Sharpness" water. By Section 15 (2) of the Gloucester and Sharpness Canal Act 1960, their abstractions from the canal were "not to exceed" as much as 25 mgd. Their Engineer, Mr Close, provided no evidence of need and did not describe 1978 as the crisis year. He did not deal with design drought conditions. The CEGB said in no uncertain terms "We are not here to say that 1978 is a crisis year." Their position is entirely fluid. 'It follows that there is a dearth of evidence to establish the SRA's first proposition: that they must have 18,000 mg of storage by 1978. You cannot drown valleys on the basis of *notional* water abstractions.'

Mr Thomas then proceeded to analyse the second proposition of the SRA, the suitability of the Dulas Valley. 'Both the River Authority and the Water Resources Board have adopted a blinkered approach – like hounds in a drag hunt.' He argued that the Authority had failed in the duties suggested to it by the Secretary of State in Parliament. They had produced no detailed evidence of the agricultural and sociological impact of the proposals and had not explored the possibility of asking independent people to assist on these issues – for example, the Radnorshire County Council, Land Agents or University Departments. Mr Inge had done his best but his references to 'a divided community' and to 'amalgamation' demonstrated that this application presented only half the picture. They treated interference with the physical environment as being on a par with interference with the social community.

What was the true picture? First, on the agricultural issues, it should not be supposed that because land is classed as Grade III or Grade IV, that it is poor or unproductive land. It is all relative to the type of farming carried out: for example, the use of bottom land with hill land. Secondly, there was ample evidence before the Inquiry as to the quality of farming in the Dulas Valley in the statement of David Daniel Jones. Geraint Howells and

Reginald Price had testified as to the quality of the stock. Councillor E. L. Evans had also stressed the size of the flocks and of the herds, and the quality of both sheep and cattle. He demonstrated pride in his valley – he was not a man scratching a living out of poor soil. Stephen Williams of the NFU had said, 'The breeding work here produces the foundation stock on which a very large pyramid of sheep production is built.' 'Is not this *first class* agricultural land?' asked Mr Thomas in summary.

The Sociological Survey might be dismissed as jargon: it had the object of examining the people of the Valley through a microscope. But the spirit of the Valley was summed up in the answer Councillor Evans gave to the Inquiry: 'It's a good place to live!' Paragraph 8.4 of the Survey described the Valley as 'a distinctive area with a marked feeling of its own'. The existence of a community there had been demonstrated in a number of ways. The bare bones were laid in Paragraph 8.7 of the Survey, but life was breathed into those bones by the farmers, the ministers, the young people and the concert which had taken place. But above all, it was the audience who had attended the Inquiry in such numbers, who were the most impressive evidence. 'These are people,' said Mr Thomas, 'who put their trust in the word of the Secretary of State. These *are* the community.'

Mr Thomas turned to consider alternative solutions. 'We recognise the problems,' he said, 'and we do not begrudge the people of the Midlands their water. We could not care less about selling it to them.' On desalinisation, he acknowledged that the prospect of cheap, desalinated water was not so immediate as to be a substitute for water storage. But there might be alternatives which would buy time until desalination became a possible solution. Estuarine barrages might be feasible, for example in the

Dee Estuary. Water treatment for polluted water was another possibility. There were sandstone acquifers in the Oswestry/Salop area and the NFU solution of a series of small reservoirs did not deserve to be dismissed because it did not solve the immediate problems. Dr Wilson's scheme was imaginative and fulfilled the stated aims of the CEGB. The proposal for the Upper Severn site should be considered also. It would provide 12.9 mgd capacity at a cost of £10 million. If the projections of demand proved to be wrong, such capacity would in any event last until 1988 and would buy time.

The capital costs of any of these projects would not be money poured down the drain. The wider social costs of drowning an inhabited valley were much more devastating. Five pence per month per family spread over sixty years was a small price to pay. The water industry, according to their Yearbook, made a capital investment each year of £60 million. £5 million additional cost, spread over the years to the late 1980s in the area of the second largest River Authority' should be viewed in that context. Dr Wilson had referred to it as a 'premium' but it was not so much a premium as a necessary economic cost. The economic price of water must now exclude the drowning of valleys. Tryweryn had demonstrated that to be true.

In conclusion, Mr Thomas said, 'It has been a privilege appearing before you, Mr Inspector. I have also had the privilege of appearing for the Councillors of Radnorshire and other local authorities. But the greatest privilege is to have spoken for the people of the Valley – and not for them only, but for their babies, for those yet unborn, for whom this land is destined as a heritage.

'You will go next week on your Inspection around this valley of theirs. You will see land tended and nurtured by generations. You will see sheep and cattle bred to the finest quality. You will meet a warm, friendly and lively community who will greet you and make you welcome.

'What will there be ten years from now? A cold, dank, silent expanse of water, the land engulfed, the community broken up and scattered?

'May God provide this thing shall never happen!'

Mr Hooson QC also thanked the Inspector in his closing speech on behalf of the Defence Committee. The approach of the Committee had been to avoid demonstrations from Valley dwellers, because they believed in the strength of their case. There was no need for shouting. It was quite clear they were opposed to site investigations leading to the construction of a reservoir. They would have an equal objection to losing their homes to a Welsh Water Board. They do not want the strength of their case marred by any difference between their case and any party political view.

The SRA had adopted a technical approach, expecting others to hire experts. Who was taking the broad view? These are issues which excite the interest of the public and give cause for anxiety. One would have expected the Water Resources Board to be doing this but it was quite patently obvious that they had not given this matter their broad attention. They had engaged in a bureaucratic process and while it was in motion, nobody stopped it to take the broad view. It was disconcerting to realise that nobody had tried to stop the machine. Mr Rowntree, called on behalf of the WRB, had said that it was the policy of the Board to avoid threats to a community wherever possible. He said the Board was prepared to pay a higher price: it was a question of balance. 'That is a confession of policy, but where is the evidence of that policy being carried out?' asked Mr Hooson. 'One alarming thing is that the capacity of the Upper Severn site was given in their glossy brochure as 4.4

mgd, but in document VR2 as 12.9 mgd, a trebling of the capacity. What was the depth of their investigation in the first place? Mr Rowntree hasn't even heard of that discrepancy. What confidence can the public have? Mr Rowntree conceded that the Upper Severn site was not even considered by the Water Resources Board. That is disconcerting. He conceded that there had been no investigation of the feasibility of water from the acquifer in the Oswestry/Salop area. He conceded that the Northern Study for the provision of a pipeline to carry water from the Dee to the Severn could give an additional source of water. This was not taken into consideration at all for satisfying the demands of the West Midlands.'

Mr Hooson continued, 'Where does this slot in? There has been a complete failure by the Water Resources Board to co-ordinate these matters. They have been at it since 1966. The evidence that they have been carrying out their declared policy is very sparse indeed. The Board's Welsh Advisory Committee said they were considering the SRA application with care: but they have never once visited the Valley. What kind of committee is it which has never been there to view the site? Two of their members have reservations. But have they considered the application properly? They have not considered the Upper Severn site at all. It is strong evidence of their inadequate approach which I am sure the Secretary of State and others will find disturbing. There is certainly no evidence that the Welsh Advisory Committee have taken any account at all of the agricultural and sociological factors. The Secretary of State must bear in mind the difference between articulating pious hopes and carrying them out. The approach of the Water Authorities and the Water Resources Board has been inadequate. They have failed to consider the application in the light of Wales and Midlands studies. For example, there have been no co-ordinated investigations involving a consideration of potential water from the Wye.'

Another issue was the lack of contingency plans. Mr Hooson pointed out that the need for such plans could arise in a number of ways: refusal of the application by the Secretary of State; snags revealed in the site investigations; or the defeat of the necessary Private Bill to implement the scheme in Parliament. Either the SRA was totally incompetent in failing to prepare contingency plans or the urgency they claimed was not there. Had the Inspector been misled? It was a very serious state of affairs and cast the gravest doubt on the SRA's own view of the 'crisis year' of 1978. If that year was so crucial, they would not have run the risk of failing to prepare contingency plans.

On the sociological issues, Mr Hooson said that it was a tragedy that publication of the 1961 Report setting out 'A' category sites seemed to have set in train a particular view. Upland reservoirs had not been fully considered. Only now was the full force of the agricultural and sociological issues being appreciated. If the Secretary of State gave his consent in the face of all of the evidence, he would be rejecting the firm opinion of his senior colleague, Tudor Watkins MP. He would be flying in the face of the representations of the social, cultural and religious leaders of the Valley and rejecting the findings of the Carter and Lewis Study. Finally, he would be jeopardising his whole position as the guardian of Welsh interests.

'This is a disturbing proposal,' concluded Mr Hooson. 'Mr Rowntree says the Water Resources Board are prepared to pay a higher price. Let's take them at their word. Let us pay the higher price and take these proposals to the Upper Severn, to a site which is completely uninhabited and where no community will be destroyed.'

The final advocate to address the Inspector was Mr Michael Mann QC for the SRA. He made an accomplished and professional closing speech, stressing the technical aspects of the proposal and the issues of cost. He gave due attention to the impact on the community, and at its conclusion, the whole audience in the Llanidloes Community Centre, who had been listening intently throughout, spontaneously applauded him for his diligence and for his courteous approach to their problems.

The Inspector then closed the public hearing and adjourned the application to enable him to carry out his physical Inspection of the Dulas Valley in the light of all the submissions he had received.

Sturdy scrub oaks firmly anchored to the upland soil, much as are the people of the Dulas Valley. Both have the right to put down roots and carry on growing.